Florida's First Families

Translated Abstracts of Pre-1821 Spanish Censuses

Volume 1

Donna Rachal Mills
Certified Genealogical Record Searcher

HERITAGE BOOKS
2011

HERITAGE BOOKS
AN IMPRINT OF HERITAGE BOOKS, INC.

Books, CDs, and more—Worldwide

For our listing of thousands of titles see our website at
www.HeritageBooks.com

Published 2011 by
HERITAGE BOOKS, INC.
Publishing Division
100 Railroad Ave. #104
Westminster, Maryland 21157

Copyright © 1992 Donna Rachal Mills

Originally published 1992
Mills Historical Press
Library of Congress Catalog Card Number 91-6661

Other books by the author:
Biographical and Historical Memoirs of Natchitoches Parish, Louisiana
Florida's Unfortunates: The 1880 Federal Census: Defective, Dependent, and Delinquent Classes
Some Southern Balls: From Valentine to Ferdinand and Beyond
The First Families of Louisiana: An Index

All rights reserved. No part of this book may be reproduced or transmitted in any form or by any means, electronic or mechanical, including photocopying, recording or by any information storage and retrieval system without written permission from the author, except for the inclusion of brief quotations in a review.

International Standard Book Numbers
Paperbound: 978-0-7884-5034-1
Clothbound: 978-0-931069-06-2

To
Elizabeth Shown Mills,
with love and much appreciation
for all she has taught me.

Table of Contents

Introduction		ix
1786	Census of St. Augustine and Its Perimeter	3
1787	Census of Householders in East Florida	34
1793	Census of St. Augustine and North River	69
1813	Census of St. Augustine, St. John's and Fernandina	111
1814	Census outside St. Augustine	123

Appendix 1:
Table of Abbreviations   152

Appendix 2:
Table of Name Conversions   153

Appendix 3:
Table of Untranslated Terms   155

Index   159

Introduction

The history of European settlement in the present United States began with Spain's discovery and subsequent colonization of Florida. At most times ignored by her beloved sovereigns, always struggling, never providing riches, the colony persisted for three centuries. By doing so, it allowed Spain a foothold in North America until the nineteenth century.

The close of the Seven Years War in 1763 wrought disastrous results for Spain and her empire; and with the signing that year of the first Treaty of Paris, she was forced to abandon her American colony. Following was Florida's only period of British rule. Her vast territory was divided into two sections, with St. Augustine serving as the control center for East Florida. With the second Treaty of Paris twenty years later, Britain not only lost her thirteen northern colonies, but her recently acquired southern province as well. Florida was again Spanish and Catholic for thirty-seven more years, an era known as the Second Spanish Period.

Although Britain had officially relinquished control of the territory in the early fall of 1783, locally the evacuation of the English government and its subjects was not to be complete for another two years. Governor Tonyon and the last 1,500 British evacuees finally withdrew from the province in September 1785. This exodus reduced Florida's population by an estimated 10,000 persons.* However, contrary to modern conceptions, as well as the peace terms that mandated total removal of all English within eighteen months, a sizeable Anglo population remained throughout the period. Loyalists fleeing the American Revolution had sought safety in the Spanish province; American frontiersman were drawn to Florida's open lands and the promise of adventure; and immigrants from England, Scotland, Ireland, Germany and Switzerland started life afresh as Spanish subjects. All had established homes (and in some cases profitable estates) during the British period, and many chose to accept Spanish authority and religion rather than abandon their property. However, the largest component of the population during the second Spanish era is known as the Menorcans—remnants of an earlier British enterprise consisting primarily of immigrants from the Balearic Islands, Greece, and Italy. Finally, a smaller group of Spaniards and native-born Floridians made up the range of "loyal" Spanish subjects co-existing in East Florida from 1794 until 1821.

Helen H. Tanner, *Zéspedes in East Florida, 1784-1790* (Tallahassee: Board of Regents of the State of Florida, 1989), xiii.

Introduction

The translated and abstracted censuses presented in this work begin with 1786—the first year following the final British removal—and end with 1814, by which time the Anglo population was once again on the increase. None are complete: portions have been lost or destroyed; military personnel (with only rare exceptions) were omitted and in some cases, families inhabiting outlying regions were originally missed or passed over. Census data varies in each according to the specific needs and purpose at the time of the counting.

The Spanish civil system varied a great deal from its Anglo counterparts, and researchers must be aware of certain customs when studying the census information. Under Spanish authorities, all females (regardless of age or nationality) were known by and recorded under their *maiden* names—a practice of vital importance to genealogists. If a female was in a second or third marriage at the taking of the census, her children of those marriages usually are listed under the deceased husband's surname, while the surname shown for their mother would ordinarily be different from those of any child or the present husband. In some cases the deceased husband or husbands are named, in others they are not. For example, the 1786 household of Edward Ashton provides the maiden name of his wife Maria (*Hinsman*), the surname of Edward's stepson by a prior marriage (*Parish*), and the surnames of Maria's children by her prior marriage (*Mott*). Neither of the deceased spouses was named.

Researchers should be thorough in following all family branches through each available census, as relevant information frequently appears amid data on relatives. For example, a researcher interested in Samuel Ashton or Inez Mott (children of Edward by his first wife and Maria Hinsman by her first husband) would find no entry on either of these children to identify the obscure parents. However, one subsequent census entry (1793) for the then-married Maria (Ashton) Fontanel, Samuel's sister, names her mother as *Dorotea Higginbothora;* and that year's entry for Isabel Mott (living with maternal relatives) cites her as the daughter of *Jonas* Mott and Maria Hindsman.

The words *Don* (D^n) and *Doña* (D^a) appear frequently throughout the censuses. These are titles of respect that can be loosely translated into *Esquire* or *Gentleman* and *Gentlewoman*. Typically, they denote members of the "upper classes," or those comparatively wealthy. Those of the highest order, such as the governor, were referred to as both *Señor* (loosely equivalent to *Mr.*) and *Don*. Finally, the Spanish census takers rarely used Anglo names, and (especially with surnames) the conversion into Spanish has often resulted in almost unrecognizable forms. Moreover, Spanish officials frequently abbreviated both the Spanish and English forms. To ease these difficulties, a list of abbreviations and a conversion table for proper names is provided in the appendices.

Introduction

The censusus abstracted and presented here are found in the collection East Florida Papers, microfilmed by the Library of Congress. Not all the lists dating to the Second Spanish Period (1783–1821) are microfilmed together on one roll or even in one series. Other censuses and census substitutes of this period, from archives of both the United States and Spain, will appear in future volumes of *Florida's First Families*.

Users should keep in mind that the records are in most cases difficult (and, in places, impossible) to read. Together with the ambiguities inherent in any translation, there exists an unavoidable margin of error. However, every attempt was made to present the material as accurately as possible. All instances of damage to or illegibility of the microfilmed original are noted.

D.R.M.

Naples, Florida
January 1992

Florida's First Families

1786

Census of St. Augustine and Its Perimeter

"Information on individuals, with exception of the Army and dependents of the Royal Hacienda, as to how many foreigners, Menorcans, Italians, Greeks, Floridians of long standing, and Spaniards, who inhabit and are found today, the nineteenth of December 1786, in this town of San Agustin in East Florida, and its perimeter to a distance of five leagues from there, with statements as to their names; native land; religion; office or occupation; age; number of their children and dependents, whether white or of color, made up in this list, and of the inquiries intended for the [page torn]... [Attested by] me, Dn. Thomas Hassett, parish curate and vicar in the above-mentioned city, on the said day, month and year."

Aliens of Different Religions and Nationalities

1.
ANA HESTER, widow, native of Georgia, Lutheran, laundress, age 32
GEREMIAS HESTER, single, native of Georgia, Lutheran, farmer, age 23
GUILLERMO OPTAN, son of the said widow, native of St. John [river] in this province, Lutheran, single, age 13

[s.1-171]

2.
D^N THOMAS JUNES[?], native of Scotland, Calvinist, merchant, single, age 24
2 female negro slaves

Source location: sheets 170 (side 2) through 206 (side 1). The numbering on the individual sheets places the sheet number after the side number—i.e., 2-170 through 1-206.

1786: St. Augustine and Its Perimeter

3.

Dᴺ JUAN HUDSON, native of Ireland, planter, Catholic, age 28
Dᴬ MARIA EVENS, native of America, Catholic, age 56
JUAN TEATS, white apprentice, native of England, convert, age 16
JORJE STEFANOPOLY, working under the above, white, native of Corsica, married with his wife absent, Catholic, age 40
DUNCAN NOBLE, native of Scotland, tailor, lives with them, Catholic, age 25
    29 male negro slaves, none baptized
    17 female negro slaves, none baptized

4.

Dᴺ FRANᶜᵒ FELIPE FACIO, native of Switzerland of the canton of Bern, planter, Catholic, age 63
Dᴬ MARIA MAGDALENA CRESPEL, his wife, native of Italy, Catholic, age 58,
Dᴬ SOPHIA FILIPINA, their daughter, native of London, single, Catholic, age 19
[s.2–171]
Dᴬ JUANA CROSS, native of New York, orphan, lives with them, convert, age 12
Dᴺ JORJE FLEMMING, native of Ireland, Catholic, merchant, lives with them, single, age 25
    5 male negro slaves, none baptized
    6 female negro slaves, none baptized

5.

Dᴺ JUAN LESLIE, native of Scotland, Protestant, merchant, single, age 35
Dᴺ JUAN FORASTER, native of America, Protestant, lives with him, single, age 20
Dᴺ JORJE CLARK, apprentice, native of this city, Catholic, age 13
    3 male negro slaves, none baptized
    7 female negro slaves, none baptized

6.

Dᴬ RICHELD BLENT, native of America, married, her husband Dⁿ Ricardo Mory absent, Lutheran, age 24
[s.1–172]
JUANA LAUREY, niece of said [Richeld], native of America, age 6
    1 male negro slave, not baptized
    1 female negro slave, not baptized

7.

Dᴬ HONORIA CLARK, widow, native of Ireland, Catholic, planter, age 40
Dᴬ MARGARITA CLARK, daughter, native of this [place], Catholic, single, age 16
[household continued on next page]

―――――――――――― 1786: St. Augustine and Its Perimeter

7. *(cont'd)*
GUALTERO WITTER, son, native of this [place], Catholic, single, age 14
Dⁿ DANIEL GRIFFIN, native of Ireland, Catholic, single, lodger of the house, age 26
THIMOTEO HOWARD Y CLAVERIA, orphan, Spanish, reared? in the house by the widow, age 11
> 8 male negro slaves
> 7 female negro slaves

[s.2-172]

8.
EDUARDO ASTHON [sic], native of Ireland, Catholic, tailor, age 38
MARIA HINSMAN, native of America, wife, age 33
JUAN PARISH, stepson of the afore-mentioned [Eduardo], native of America, single, convert, farmer, age 17
SAMUEL, son of the afore-mentioned [Eduardo] and his first wife, convert, age 13
FELIPE, son of the afore-mentioned [Eduardo] and his first wife, convert, age 12
JULIANA, daughter of the afore-mentioned [Eduardo] and his first wife, convert, age 11
EDUARDO, son of the said [Eduardo] and his first wife, convert, age 9
ISABELA MOTT, daughter of the above-mentioned Catholic, Maria Hinsman, native of this [place], Catholic, age 11
INES MOTT, daughter of the said Maria and first husband, as is the before-mentioned Isabela, native of this [place], Catholic, age 9

9.
MARIA HAZARD, native of America, widow, Protestant, age 45
ISABELA PERRY, her daughter, native of America, Protestant, married, her husband absent, age 25

[s.1-173]

MARIA PERRY, daughter, native of this [place], Catholic, single, age 13
ENRIQUE MAYRO, son of Isabela Perry, native of this [place], age 4
REGINA MARGARITA WHITE, widow, native of Prussia, Protestant, lives with them, age 65

10.
MARIA COLLEN, married, her husband absent, native of America, Protestant, age 35
ANA, daughter, native of America, age 8
MARIA LUISA RODRIGUES, native of America, Catholic, widow, age 27
JOSEPH MARIA DE JESUS GERON VILLAN, son of the said [Maria Luisa], native of Mobile, Catholic, age 11

1786: St. Augustine and Its Perimeter

11.
JORJE BACHOS, native of Bengal [India], Protestant, single, tailor, age 37
MARIA HARRIS, mulatto slave of the said [Jorje], Protestant, age 40

[s.2-173]

12.
THOMAS CORDERY, native of America, butcher, Protestant, age 64
MARIA LEASEWELL, native of America, wife, of the same religion, age 59
ESTEVAN, son, native of this [place], of the same religion, single, age 16
SARA MORPHY, granddaughter of [Thomas and Maria], native of America, age 5
CATARINA MORIN, native of America, Protestant, single, age 24

13.
BARBARA STRASBURG, widow, native of Germany, Catholic, farmer, age 60
MARGARITA HINSMANT, daughter, native of America, single, Catholic, age 27
INES HINSMANT, daughter, native of America, single, Catholic, age 24

[s.1-174]

14.
SANTIAGO CLARK, native of Scotland, tavern keeper, Protestant, age 31
MARGARITA CZERICH, his wife, of the same religion, age 48
JAYME TEATS, white apprentice, single, Protestant, age 14
    1 female slave, not baptized
    3 male negro servants, none baptized

15.
JUAN HYQUINS, native of England, Protestant, shoemaker, age 35
ISABEL MᶜMULLEN, his wife, native of Scotland, Protestant, age 42
GROVES DORAN, native of Ireland, Catholic, shoemaker, lives with them, age 40

[s.2-174]

16.
BARBARA JAYSMEN SIMPSON, widow, native of Pennsylvania, Catholic, age 33
ANNA, daughter, native of this [place], age 11
FELIPE, son, native of this [place], age 4

17.
ANTONIO HINSMAN, native of America, Catholic, farmer, age 36
LEONORA GENOPLEY, his wife, native of America, Catholic, age 19
MARIA BARBARA, daughter, native of this [place], age 5 months
INES ANA ANTONIA, daughter of unknown parents, cared for by said Leonora, age 1 month

―――――――――――― 1786: St. Augustine and Its Perimeter

17. *(cont'd)*
JUAN LY, native of America, Protestant, farmer, single, lives with them, age 20

[s.1-175]

18.
JORJE HINSMAN, native of America, farmer, Catholic, age 33
MARIA ISABELA, wife, native of America, Catholic, age 18

19.
JAYME M^CGIRT, native of Carolina, farmer, Lutheran, age 50
ISABELA SANDERS, his wife, native of the same and of the same religion, age 43
JAYME, son, native of the same, single, farmer, age 20
JUAN, son, native of the same, single, farmer, age 18
ESACARIAS, son, native of the same, single, farmer, age 16
DANIEL, son, native of the same, single, farmer, age 14
ROBERTO, son, native of the same, single, farmer, age 12
MARIA, daughter, native of the same, age 10
    —all of the same religion
    4 male negro slaves
    2 female negro slaves

[s.2-175]

20.
JOSEPH HUES, native of London, farmer, Lutheran, widower, age 56
JOSEPH, son, native of the same, single, farmer, of the same religion, age 15
GEREMIAS HESTER, native of Georgia, farmer, single, Protestant, lives with them, age 21
LUIS, native of America, lives with them, farmer, Protestant, age 13

21.
RANDOLPH MACDONELL, native of Scotland, Catholic, farmer, single, age 45
ALEXANDRO MAGDONEL [*sic*], native of the same, single, farmer, Catholic, age 26
    4 male slaves, none baptized
    2 female slaves, none baptized

[s.1-176]

22.
DEOPHUS HILL, native of America, Protestant, farmer, age 43
THERESA THOMASA, his wife, native of the same and of the same religion, age 41
SARA, daughter, native of the same, single, of the same religion, age 15
    [household continued on next page]

1786: St. Augustine and Its Perimeter

22. (cont'd)

CHRISCHEANY [CHRISTINA] HILL, daughter, native of the same, single, of the same religion, age 12

MARIA, daughter, native of the same, and of the same religion, age 8

ISABELA, daughter, native of the same, of the same religion, age 5

      7 male slaves, none baptized
      4 female slaves, none baptized

23.

D^N GEREMIAS FIS [FISH], native of New York, planter, Protestant, married, his wife absent, age 54

GEREMIAS, son, native of this [place], of the same religion as his father, absent, age 7

[s. 2-176]

      7 male slaves, not baptized
      7 female slaves, not baptized

DIEGO, free negro male living with them, Catholic [*no age given*]

Totals:

Married Couples of this Category	13
White Males	47
White Females	38
Total White Persons	85
Male Negroes	72
Female Negroes	54
Total Negro Persons	126
Total	211

Note By Hassett:
"To this total has been added one male Indian and one female mulatto, which makes two hundred and thirteen."

─────────────── 1786: St. Augustine and Its Perimeter

Menorquians, Italians, Greeks, and Others Known as Such

[s.1-177]

1.
JOSEPH PONS, of Menorca, farmer, age 33
MARIANA RUGERA, his wife, Menorcan, age 50
ANTONIA VENS, daughter of the said Mariana and another husband, of Mosquitos, single, age 14
GERONIMO ALVAREZ, Spanish, baker, lives with them, age 27
JUAN TAYLOR, native of America, Protestant, farmer, lives with them, age 21
    2 negro slaves of the said Alvarez, not baptized

2.
FERDINANDO FALANY, Italian, farmer, age 42
MARGARITA VELORY, his wife, a Maonesa [of Mayna], age 34

[s.2-177]

MARIA, daughter, of Mosquitos, age 9
SANTIAGO, son, of this [place], age 6
THERESA, daughter, of this [place], age 1
GUILLERMO, free mulatto, American, Protestant, lives with them, age 20

3.
LUCIA PESO DE BURGO, widow, of Corsica, age 40
PEDRO, her son, of Mosquitos, age 12

4.
PABLO VILLA, native of France, baker, single, age 35

5.
JOSEPH ROSY, native of Italy, farmer, age 45
FRAN^CA, his wife, of Menorca, age 40
MARGARITA, daughter, of Mosquitos, single, age 16
ANGELA, daughter, of Mosquitos, age 10
FRANCISCA, daughter, of this [place], age 7

[s.1-178]

GASPAR, son, of this [place], age 4
JOSEPH, son, age three months

6.
MAGDALENA RUGERA, widow, of Menorca, age 46
BARTHOLOMEO SIENTES, her son, of Menorca, single, tailor, age 23

9

1786: St. Augustine and Its Perimeter

7.
MARTIN HERNANDEZ, of Menorca, carpenter, age 30
DOROTEA GOMILLA, his wife, of Menorca, age 24
MARGARITA, their daughter, of this [place], age 3
CATARINA, daughter, of this [place], age 1
FRANCISCO MARIN, white apprentice, carpenter, of Mosquitos, age 15
JUAN ALCINA, white apprentice, of Menorca, age 22
JOSEPH GOMILLA, widower, father of said Dorotea, of Menorca, fisherman, lives with them, age 50
JUAN HEARN^z, of Menorca, carpenter, single, age 24
GASPAR HERNANDEZ, of Menorca, porter, single, age 22

[s.2-178]

JOSEPH HERNANDEZ, of Menorca, carpenter, single, age 20
    2 male slaves, one Christian
    1 female slave, Christian

8.
BARTOLOMEO LOPEZ, of Menorca, farmer, age 30
MARIANA ALBARTY, his wife, of Menorca, age 30
CRISTOVAL, son, of this [place], age 5
ANDRES, son, of this [place], age 3
JUAN REYES, of Mosquitos, lives with them, age 10
ANDRES LOPEZ, of Menorca, farmer, lives with them, single, age 23
JUANA, daughter of Bartolomeo and of Mariana, of this [place], age 10 months
    1 female negro slave, not baptized

9.
DIEGO HERNANDEZ, of Menorca, farmer, age 45
VICTORIA VIVAS, his wife, of Menorca, age 46
DIEGO, son, of Menorca, mariner, single, age 26

[s.1-179]

ANTONIO, son, of Mosquitos, single, cooper[?], age 15
AGUEDA, daughter, of Mosquitos, age 11

10.
ANTONIO JOSEPH ALBERTI, of Menorca, farmer, age 37
CATARINA OLIBER[AS], his wife, of Menorca, age 33
CRISTOVAL, son, of Mosquitos, age 14
MARIA, daughter, of Mosquitos, age 11
JUAN, son, of this [place], age 7
FRANCISCA, daughter, of this [place], age 4
JUANA MARIA, daughter, of this [place], age 1 month
MARIA MAGDALENA GAVARDY, daughter of said Catarina and another husband, of Mosquitos, single, age 15

1786: St. Augustine and Its Perimeter

[s.2-179]

11.
ANTONIO ANDRES, of Menorca, carpenter, age 36
AGUEDA PONS, his wife, of Menorca, age 34
JUAN, their son, of Mosquitos, age 12
ANTONIO, son, of this [place], age 6
MAGDALENA, daughter, of this [place], age 1
JUANA PONS, of Menorca, single, living with them, age 21
DOMINGO BALS, of Mosquitos, white apprentice, single, carpenter, age 15

12.
ANTONIO ALCINA, of Menorca, farmer, age 40
RAFAELA CAPO, his wife, of Menorca, age 33
MIGUEL, son of Antonio and first wife, of Mosquitos, single, farmer, age 14
CATARINA, daughter of the above two, of this [place], age 6
RAFAELA, daughter, of this [place], age 4
ANTONIA, daughter, of this [place], age 1

[s.1-180]

1 female slave, not baptized

13.
PASQUAL SANS, of Naples, mariner, age 40
ANTONIA FERNARIS, his wife, of Menorca, age 32
JUANA, daughter, of Mosquitos, single, age 14

14.
DOMINGO ESCERCOPORY DEL BRAZO, of Mayna, carpenter, age 30
GERONIMA IBARNAU, his wife, of Menorca, age 40

15.
PEDRO RODRIGUES, of the Canary Islands, tavern keeper, single, age 30

16.
DIEGO SEGUY, of Menorca, farmer, age 40
JUANA CASTELL, his wife, of Menorca, age 31

[s.2-180]

MARIA, daughter, of this [place], age 9
JUANA, daughter, of this [place], age 18 months

17.
BARTOLOMEO FILLERA, of Menorca, farmer, age 36
JUANA HERNAU, his wife, of Menorca, age 34
MIGUEL, son, of this [place], age 8
DIEGO, son, of this [place], age 5
JUANA, daughter, of this [place], age 2

1786: St. Augustine and Its Perimeter

18.
JOSEPH AGLES, of Menorca, farmer, age 56
MARIA FONS, his wife, of Menorca, age 50
FRANCISCO FONS, farmer, lives with them, age 32

19.
VIZENTE BARDORON, of France, mariner, single, age 26

JOSEPH TORDO, of Italy, mariner, single, age 25

[s.1-181]

20.
JOSEPH PESO DE BURGO, of Corsica, shopkeeper, single, age 30
FRANCISCO PRAIS, dependent of said [Joseph], of Mosquitos, single, age 14
    1 male negro slave, not baptized
    1 female negro slave, not baptized

21.
JUAN GLODO [CLAUDE?] BODLAM, hatter, single, of France, age 25

22.
JOSEPH PONS Y TRIAY, of Menorca, farmer, age 52
MARGARITA TRIAY, his wife, of Menorca, age 50
DIMAS, son, of this [place], age 4
ANTONIO LEDO, single, lives with them, farmer, from Portugal, age 55
    1 female slave, baptized

[s.2-181]

23.
ANTONIO CANTAR, of Menorca, boat master, age 32
CATARINA ACOSTA, his wife, of Corsica, age 26
AGUSTIN, their son, of Mosquitos, age 11
DOMINGO, son, of this [place], age 6
MARIA, daughter, of this [place], age 2
PATRICIO, son, of this [place], age 6 months
    2 female slaves, not baptized
    1 free male negro, lives with them

24.
JUAN BAPTISTA PAYERES, of Mallorca, mariner, age 31
ISABELA RIDABET, his wife, of Menorca, age 28
JUANA, daughter, of this [place], age 18 months
JUAN JOSEF ECHAUARRIA, lives with them, tailor, of Spain, 32

─────────────── 1786: St. Augustine and Its Perimeter

25.
JUAN FRAN^{co} ARNAU, mariner, of France, age 28
ISABELA MULA, his wife, of Menorca, age 32
[s.1-182]
JUANA MARGO, daughter of Isabela and first husband, of this [place], age 7
ISABELA, daughter of [first] above-mentioned couple, of this [place], age 2

26.
ANTONIO CANOBAS, native of Menorca, farmer, age 30
CATARINA MAESTRE, his wife, of Menorca, age 26
ANTONIO, son, of this [place], age 4

27.
FRANCISCO BAUSA, mariner, of Mallorca, age 28
EULALIA OLIVAS, his wife, of Menorca, age 48 [sic]
PEREGRY GRYNALDY, single son of the said Eulalia and another husband, of Mosquitos, age 15
SPIRION GRYNALDY, son of the said [Eulalia] and another husband, age 9
FRANCISCA PONCELLA, married, her husband absent, of Menorca, lives with them, age 25
[s.2-182]
MARIA MAGDALENA, daughter of the said [Francisca], of this [place], age 5

28.
FRANCISCO STACOLY [ESTACHOLY], mariner, of Liorna, age 26
MARIA PETROS, his wife, of Menorca, age 37
DOMINGO, son, of Mosquitos, single, age 13
BARTOLOMEO, son, of Mosquitos, age 11
BARBARA, daughter, of this [place], age 4

29.
JUAN BALUM, tavern keeper, single, of Menorca, age 29
LORENZO COLL, mariner, single, of Mallorca, age 40

30.
JULIANA COLLENS, of New Orleans, Catholic, age 43
[s.1-183]
JUAN BAUTISTA, free mulatto of New Orleans, Catholic, trader, age 23
JULIANA JAABYT, native of America, her religion Anglican, single, age 26
ROSA, negro slave of the said Juliana, not baptized, age 14

31.
ANTONIA ROGIER, widow, of Menorca, age 60
ANTONIO MESTRE, her son, of Menorca, widower, farmer, age 36

1786: St. Augustine and Its Perimeter

32.
ROQUE LEONARDI, farmer, of Italy, age 44
AGUEDA COLL, his wife, of Menorca, age 36
JOSEPHA CIROLINDA, daughter, of Mosquitos, age 11
JUAN, son, of this [place], age 7

[s.2–183]

BARTOLOMEO, son, of this [place], age 5
JACOBA, daughter, of this [place], age 5 months
JUAN CHATO, son of the said Agueda and another husband, age 15
    1 female negro slave, converted
    1 free negro male, not baptized

33.
LUIS BUCHENTINY, farmer, of Liorna, age 39
CATARINA COLL, his wife, of Menorca, age 24
JOSEPH BATELINY, single, farmer, of Italy, age 40

34.
SEVASTIAN ESTEVE, of France, jailor, age 50
JUANA SALON, his wife, of Menorca, age 33
FRANCISCO, son, of this [place], age 7
JUAN, son, of this [place], age 3
CATARINA, daughter, of this [place], age 6
JUANA, daughter, of this [place], age 10 days

[s.1–184]

35.
BERNARDO SEGUY, of Menorca, trader, age 44
AGUEDA VILLALONGA, his wife, of Menorca, age 33
AGUEDA, daughter, of Mosquitos, age 11
ANTONIA, daughter, of Mosquitos, age 9
CLARA, daughter, of this [place], age 7
BARTOLOMEO, son, of this [place], age 6
BLANCA, daughter, of this [place], age 4
BERNARDO, son, of this [place], age 2
    1 male negro, not baptized
    2 female negroes, not baptized

36.
JUAN SOLON, of Menorca, farmer, age 35
MARGARITA NETO, his wife, of Menorca, age 29
JUAN, son, of this [place], age 7
CLARA, daughter, of this [place], age 4
    1 male negro, not baptized
    2 female negroes, not baptized

―――――――――――― 1786: St. Augustine and Its Perimeter

37.
ANTONIA PETROS, of Menorca, married, her husband absent, age 28

38.
VIZENTE CARELLI, of Menorca, carpenter, age 36
CATARINA RITA VENS, his wife, of Menorca, age 50 [sic]
AGUEDA, daughter, of Mosquitos, age 14
PEDRO, son, of Mosquitos, age 11
    1 female negro, not baptized

[s.2-184]

39.
GASPAR PAPE, of Esmerna [Smyrna], farmer, age 36
ANA PONS, his wife, of Menorca, age 24

40.
NICOLAS ESTEVANOPOLY, of Corsica, carpenter, age 38
JUANA MARIN, his wife, of Menorca, age 31
MALTA, daughter, of Mosquitos, age 11
JUANA, daughter, of this [place], age 4
FRANCISCO, son, of this [place], age 6 months

41.
JUAN JEONADA, of Menorca, farmer, age 36
MAGDALENA MARIN, his wife, of Menorca, age 28
MAGDALENA, daughter, of this [place], age 4
FRAN^{co}, son, of this [place], age 1

[s.1-185]

42.
ANGELINO BACHERI, of Liorna, mariner, age 34
JOSEFA CASTELL, his wife, of Menorca, age 36
BARTOLOMEO, their son, of Mosquitos, age 12
PEDRO, son, of Mosquitos, age 10
CATARINA, daughter, of this [place], age 7

43.
JUAN QUEVEDO, of Menorca, tailor, age 24
JUANA SEGUY, his wife, of Mosquitos, age 15
IGNES VICTORI, widow, of Menorca, lives with them, age 56
FRAN^{co} PUELLA, of Havana, apprentice, single, white, tailor, age 14
    1 female negro, not baptized

1786: St. Augustine and Its Perimeter

44.
SEVASTIAN ORTEGAS, of Menorca, mariner, age 33
ANA MARIA QUEVEDO, his wife, of Menorca, age 37
SEVASTIAN, son, of Mosquitos, age 12
SANTIAGO, son, of Mosquitos, age 9
BERNARDO, son, of this [place], age 6 months
ANA MARIA, daughter, of this [place], age 3

[s.2-185]

45.
JUAN FESUA, of Menorca, mariner, age 36
AGUEDA, his wife, of Menorca, age 30

46.
LORENZO CAPOT, widower, of Menorca, sacristan, age 40
RAFAELA, daughter, of this [place], age 5
ANTONIO, son, of this [place], age 3
    3 free male negroes, not baptized
    4 free female negroes, not baptized

47.
ISABELA PRAS Y PEPOD, married, her husband absent, of Menorca, age 40
JUAN PEPALL, son, single, trader, of Menorca, age 24
GABRIEL, son, single, trader, of Menorca, age 20
MARIA GARCIA, daughter, single, of this [place], age 15
    4 male slaves, not baptized
    5 female negro slaves, not baptized

[s.1-186]

48.
JUANA PERPAL, married, her husband absent, of Menorca, age 22
DOMINGO, her son, of this [place], age 7
    1 female slave, not baptized

49.
AGUEDA VILLALONGA, widow, of Menorca, age 50
MARTINA [no surname given], granddaughter, of this [place], age 6

50.
BARTOLOMEO LAUFRIO, of Menorca, farmer, age 33
ANTONIA MAESTRE, his wife, of Menorca, age 30
BARTOLOMEO, son, of this [place], age 5
URSULA, daughter, age 2

[s.2-186]

1786: St. Augustine and Its Perimeter

51.
DOMINGO MARTINOLY, of Italy, mariner, age 30
MARIANA QUEVEDO, his wife, of Menorca, age 21
JUAN, son, of this [place], age 5
SANTIAGO, son, of this [place], age 3
PETRONA, daughter, of this [place], age 1
    1 male negro slave, not baptized
    1 female negro slave, Catholic

52.
JUANA HERNANDEZ, widow, of Menorca, age 50
RAFAEL HERNANDEZ, single, son, of Menorca, tailor, age 24

53.
BARTHOLOME PELIGRI, native of Menorca, mariner, age 22
JUANA HERNANDEZ, his wife, of Menorca, age 22
ANTONIA, daughter, of this [place], age 3

[s.1-187]

54.
SEBASTIAN COLL, of Menorca, carpenter, age 29
MARGARITA VILLA, his wife, of Menorca, age 23
SEVASTIAN COLL, son, of this [place], age 5
PEDRO COLL, son, of this [place], age 1

55.
ANDRES PACETI, native of Leonia [Liorna?], farmer, age 36
MARIA CASTELL, his wife, of Menorca, age 26
CLARA MARIA, daughter of the said Andres and first wife, native of St. Augustine, age 14
THOMAS, son of the said Andres and first wife, of this [place], age 12
MAGDALENA daughter of Andres and first wife, of this [place], age 8

[s.2-187]

GETRUDIS ROSA, daughter of Andres and first wife, of this [place], age 5
AGATA SEGUY, daughter of said Maria Castell and her first husband, of this [place], age 3
ANDRES DAECTE, son of the said couple, age 6 months
    1 male negro slave, not baptized

56.
PEDRO COUFACI, native of Corsica, trader, age 36
INES QUEVEDO, his wife, of Menorca, age 36
MARIA ROSA GINERINI, daughter of said Ines and first husband, of this [place], age 11

[household continued on next page]

1786: St. Augustine and Its Perimeter

56. (cont'd)
INES GINERINI, daughter of said Ines and first husband, of this [place], age 10
MARTA, daughter of the said couple, of this [place], age 6
PAREDIS, daughter, of this [place], age 4
   2 male & 2 female negro slaves, not baptized

57.
FRANCISCO SEGUI, of Menorca, mariner, age 36

[s.1-188]

ISABELA MORA, his wife, of Menorca, age 32
JUANA MARIA, daughter, of Mosquitos, age 12
AGATA MARIA, daughter, of Mosquitos, age 9

58.
JUAN VILLA, of Menorca, weaver[?], age 40
MARIA ANNA CARDONA, his wife, of Menorca, age 35
MARGARITA, daughter, of Mosquitos, age 11
MARIA ANNA, daughter, of this [place], age 7
AGATA, daughter, of this [place], age 6
   2 male & 2 female negro slaves, not baptized

59.
MANUEL PONS, of Menorca, taverner and farmer, age 36
JUANA VILLA, his wife, of Menorca, age 30
ANTONIA, daughter, of this [place], age 5

[s.2-188]

AGATA, daughter, of this [place], age 3
FRANCISCO, son, of this [place], age 9 months
MARIA, slave, converted

60.
ANTONIO BERTA, of Italy, taverner, age 25
MARIANA ZANS, his wife, of Menorca, age 20
CATARINA MIR, daughter of Mariana and first spouse, of this [place], age 3
MICHAELA MIR, daughter of Mariana and first spouse, of this [place], age 9 mos.
   1 female negro slave, Catholic

61.
MIGUEL SEGUI, of Menorca, carpenter, age 36
CLARA ROSARIO, his wife, of Menorca, age 37
MARGARITA, daughter, of Mosquitos, single, age 13
MAGDALENA, daughter, of Mosquitos, age 11
CLARA, daughter, of Mosquitos, age 9
JUANA, daughter, of Mosquitos, age 6
NICOLAS, son, of Mosquitos, age 3

1786: St. Augustine and Its Perimeter

[s.1-189]

62.

JOSEPH BUCHONI, of Italy, mariner, age 39
MARIA COSTA, his wife, of Menorca, age 30
MARIA MAURIRY, daughter of said Maria and first husband, of Mosquitos, age 11
MIGUEL MAURIRI, son of Maria and first husband, of this [place], age 7

63.

NICOLAS NICOLIK, of Italy, mariner, age 40
JOSEPHA COLL, his wife, of Menorca, age 30
JOSEPHA FEMENIAS, daughter of the said Josepha and first husband, age 11
MARTIN, son of the said couple of this [place], age 2

[s.2-189]

JUAN BARBER, native of Menorca, single, mariner, lives with them, age 25

64.

MARCOS ANDRES, of Menorca, mariner, age 26
MARIANA FUESLINY, his wife, of Menorca, age 28
ANTONIO POSILL, son of said Mariana and first husband, of this [place], age 7
MARCOS, son of said couple, of this [place], age 4
ANTONIA, daughter, of this [place], age 2
RAFAEL, son, of this [place], age 6 months

65.

FRANCISCO PALLERIN [sic], of Menorca, age 39
JUANA VILLA, his wife, of Menorca, age 22

[s.1-190]

ANTONIO PELLICER, son of Francisco and first wife, of Mosquitos, age 12
JUANA PELLICER, daughter of said Francisco and first wife, of Mosquitos, age 10
MARIA, daughter of said couple [Francisco and Juana], of this [place], age 2
    1 female negro slave, not baptized

66.

SANTIAGO PRAST, of Menorca, farmer, age 50
MARGARITA VIVAS, native of Menorca, his wife, age 37
BENEDITA ALCINA, daughter of Bartolomeo, lives with them, age 14

67.

MARIA TRIAY, widow, of Menorca, age 50
FRANCISCO TRIAY, widower, of Menorca, farmer, age 36

[s.2-190]

    2 male negro slaves
    2 female negro slaves, baptized

1786: St. Augustine and Its Perimeter

68.
JUAN TRIAY, of Menorca, farmer, age 32
JUANA XIMENES, his wife, of Menorca, age 35
JOSEPH BAYA, son of said Juana and first husband, of this [place], age 9
JUAN TRIAY, son of the said [Juan and Juana], age 5
FRANCISCO, son, of this [place], age 4
GUILLERMO, son, of this [place], age 2
    1 male negro slave, not baptized

69.
JOSEPH CARRERES, of Menorca, farmer, age 31
JUANA ANDREA, his wife, of Menorca, age 40
MARIA, daughter, of this [place], age 5
JUAN, son, of this [place], age 7 months
DOMINGO VALS, son of said Juana and first husband, of Mosquitos, single, age 15

[s.1-191]

DIEGO CARRERES, of Menorca, single, shipwright, lives with them, age 25

70.
RAFAEL XIMENES, of Menorca, farmer, age 50
MARIA RAMALERA, his wife, of Menorca, age 35
MARIA, daughter, of this [place], age 7
ESPERANZA, daughter, of this [place] age 4
CATARINA, daughter of this [place], age 2
    1 male negro slave, not baptized

71.
ANTONIO TUDIDICHO, of Italy, mariner, single, age 40
ANA IACENS [YACENS?], married, with her husband absent, Catholic, of Ireland, age 32

[s.2-191]

72.
DOMETRIO TUDIDACHE [sic], mariner, of Italy, age 40
MARIA BRAUS, his wife, of Lanturin, age 50
MIGUEL COSTA, son of Maria and another husband, of Corsica, age 24
JORJE COSTA, son of Maria and another husband, of Corsica, age 20
NICOLAS, son of said couple [Dometrio and Maria], of Mosquitos, mariner, age 14

73.
JOSEPH ESPINETE, of Menorca, fisherman, age 40
MARIA TREAL, his wife, of Menorca, age 48
FRANCISCO, son, of Mosquitos, age 13

1786: St. Augustine and Its Perimeter

74.
FRAN^co MARIN, shoemaker, of Catalonia, age 65
MAGDALENA ESCUDERO, his wife, of Menorca, age 53
ANTONIO LEMBRAS, carpenter, living with them, of Menorca, age 25
JORJE MEDECHY, grandson of Marin, single, of Mosquitos, age 13
MAGDALENA MEDECHY, granddaughter of said Marin, of Mosquitos, age 9
FRANCISCO [no surname given], grandson of said Marin, of this [place], age 5
ELIAS MEDECHY, widower, of Corsica, shoemaker, age 36

[s.1–192]

75.
JUAN TENEVARDY, farmer, of Menorca, age 46
ANTONIA MORILLA, his wife, of Menorca, age 36
FRAN^co, son of said Juan and first wife, mariner, single, of Mallorca, age 22
MARTIN PELLICER, son of said Antonia and first husband, of Menorca, age 20
MARGARITA, daughter of the couple [Juan and Antonia], of this [place], age 5
JUANA, daughter, of this [place], age 3
MARIA ANTONIA, daughter, of this [place], age 2 months

[p.2–192]

76.
JUAN IENOCLY, widower, carpenter, of Mayna, age 36
PEDRO DIMALACHY, carpenter, widower, of Corsica, age 38
MARIA, daughter of said Pedro, single, of Mosquitos, age 13
NICOLAS, son of said Pedro, of this [place], age 7
    2 male negro slaves, not baptized
    1 female slave, not baptized

77.
MARGARITA GUIBARNAU, married, her husband absent, of Menorca, age 38
ANA CAPELE, daughter, of Mosquitos, age 12
FRANCISCO, son, of this [place], age 6

78.
FRANCISCO ARNAU, mariner, of Menorca, age 40
CLARA PRETA, his wife, of Menorca, age 36
FRAN^ca, daughter, single, of Mosquitos, age 14
ANTONIA, daughter, of Mosquitos, age 12
SANTIAGO, son, of Mosquitos, age 10
FRANCISCA, daughter, of Mosquitos, age 6

[s.1–193]

1786: St. Augustine and Its Perimeter

79.
MIGUEL VILLALONGA, farmer, of Menorca, age 29
RAFAELA MERCADAL, his wife, of Menorca, age 26
AGUEDA, daughter, of this [place], age 5
RAFAELA, daughter, of this [place], age 2
FRANCISCA, daughter, of this [place], age 3 months

80.
JUAN CARERAS, carpenter, of Menorca, age 40
MARIA TRIAY, his wife, of Menorca, age 21
MARGARITA, daughter, of this [place], age 1 and one day

[s.2-193]

81.
JUAN SEGUY, farmer, of Menorca, age 30
AGUEDA ENNRIQUE, his wife, of Menorca, age 24
BENITO, son, of this [place], age 2
MATHEO, son, of this [place], age 3 months

82.
PEDRO FEZUA, farmer, of Menorca, age 30
FRANCISCA PRETOS, his wife, of Menorca, age 29

83.
JUAN LORENZO, bricklayer, of Menorca, age 31
MARIA VILLA, his wife, of Menorca, age 28
MARIANA, daughter, of this [place], age 7
JUAN, son, of this [place], age 5
FRANCISCO, son, of this [place], age 3
ANTONIA, daughter, of this [city], age 1

[s.1-194]

84.
JUANA MARIA ALBERTINY, married, [her husband] with military, of Menorca, age 33
CRISTOVAL REYES, son of Juana and her first husband, single, of Mosquitos, age 14
JUAN REYES, son of Juana and first husband, of Mosquitos, age 10
MARIANA, daughter of Juana and first husband, of this [place], age 8
CATARINA, daughter of Juana and first husband, of this [place], age 6

85.
FRANCISCO DEL MEDO, mariner, of Menorca, age 36
JUANA VENS, his wife, of Menorca, age 26

[s.2-194]

1786: St. Augustine and Its Perimeter

85. (cont'd)
PEDRO, son, of this [place], age 2
ANA MARIA, daughter, of this [place], age 6 days

86.
ANA FERRER [FERREN?], widow, of Menorca, age 60
PEDRO LUET, nephew of Ana, widower, mariner, of Menorca, age 40

87.
JOSEPH ARNAU, farmer, of Menorca, age 24
ANA AGORNES, his wife, of Mosquitos, age 17

88.
PABLO SABALT, farmer, of Menorca, age 25
ANTONIA ORTEGAS, his wife, of Menorca, age 23
MIGUEL, son, of this [place], age 2
CATARINA, daughter, of this [place], age 3 months
ANA CERES GONZALES, widow, of Menorca, lives with them, age 47
PEDRO ESUA, single, farmer, of Menorca, lives with them, age 36
    1 male negro slave, not baptized

[s.1-195]

89.
JUAN TRIAY PONS, fisherman, of Menorca, age 40
ANTONIA TRIAY, his wife, of Menorca, age 38
JUANA [TRIAY?],* daughter of said Antonia and another husband, of Mosquitos, age 11
ANTONIO [TRIAY?],* son of said Antonia and first husband, single, of Mosquitos, age 13 [sic]
    2 male negro slaves
    2 female negro slaves, not baptized

[s.2-195]

90.
PEDRO OSIAS, mariner, of France, age 36
MARIA ORTEGAS, his wife, of Menorca, age 26
PEDRO, son, of this [place], age 4
ANA, daughter, of this [place], age 1

---

* It is probable that the surname is *not* Triay. This enumerator lists females by maiden name, and the odds are small that the former husband was a Triay also.

1786: St. Augustine and Its Perimeter

91.
JOSEPH HERNANDEZ, bricklayer, of Menorca, age 40
MARIA MIER, his wife, of Menorca, age 27
MARTINA, daughter, of Mosquitos, single, age 12
CATARINA, daughter, of this [place], age 7
JOSEPH, son, of this [place], age 4
MARIA, daughter, of this [place], age 1 year and 6 months
GABRIEL, son, of this [place], age 7 months
    3 male black slaves
    4 female black slaves

[s.1-196]

92.
LORENZO CAPELA, fisherman, of Menorca, age 23
GERONIMA, daughter, of this [place], age 4 months

93.
JOSEPH HERNANDEZ, married, farmer, of Menorca, age 40
JUANA LLINA, his wife, of Menorca, age 50
JUAN RIMA, son of said Juana and first husband, single, fisherman, of Menorca, age 21

94.
JORJE CLAK, mariner, of Menorca, age 30

[s.2-196]

INEZ PABLO, his wife, of Menorca, age 30
PEDRO DURANTE, son of Inez and first husband, of Mosquitos, age 17
ANDRES BRON, son of the said couple [Jorje and Inez], of this [place], age 4
JORJE CLAK, son, of this [place], age 10 months
ANTONIA CLAK, single, native of Menorca, lives with them, age 50

95.
LUIS SOCHE, mariner, of Italy, age 48
ANTONIA TREMOL, his wife, of Menorca, age 28
FRANCISCO TREMOL, mariner, single, lives with them, of Menorca, age 24

96.
GABRIEL TRIAY, carpenter, of Menorca, age 30
MARGARITA PONS [SANZ?], his wife, of Menorca, age 25

[s.1-197]

ANTONIO, son, of this [place], age 4
GABRIEL, son, of this [place], age 6 months

1786: St. Augustine and Its Perimeter

97.
ALBERTO RUGER, shipwright, of Menorca, age 31
ANTONIA VILLA, his wife, of Menorca, age 26
CATALINA, daughter, of this [place], age 3
RAMON, son, of this [place], age 1

98.
ANTONIO ROYO, farmer, of Menorca, widower, age 35
ANTONIA, daughter, of Mosquitos, age 17
    1 male negro slave
    1 female negro slave

[s.2-197]

99.
MATEO PELEGRINO, farmer, of Leorna, age 36
ANA MARIA PELLEGRINO, his wife, of Menorca, age 30
FERNANDO, son of said Mateo and first wife, of Mosquitos, age 11
MARIA, daughter of the said couple [Matheo and Ana], age 2

100.
JOACHIN MACHIOCHI, mariner, of Italy, age 32
MAGDALENA [no surname], his wife, of Menorca, age 26
JUAN, son, of Mosquitos, age 12
JUAN PONS, of Mosquitos, lives with them, age 14
MARGARITA PONS, of Mosquitos, lives with them, age 11

101.
JUAN PONS, farmer, of Menorca, age 25
JUANA ANDREU, his wife, of Mosquitos, age 14

[s.1-198]

102.
GUILLERMO M^cPRENY, widower, of Ireland, maintained as a Menorcan, trader, 47

103.
PEDRO ESTOPA, of Menorca, farmer, age 36
ANA QUINTANA, his wife, of Menorca, age 42
MARGARITA, daughter of said Pedro and first wife, single, of Mosquitos, age 12

104.
ANA TURAN, widow, of Menorca, age 60
PEDRO TRIAY, son, farmer, of Menorca, age 31
GABRIEL TURAN, brother of said [Ana], mariner, of Menorca, age 46

[s.2-198]

1786: St. Augustine and Its Perimeter

105.
JUAN CAPO, farmer, of Menorca, age 54
AGUEDA SEGUERA, his wife, of Menorca, age 50
PEDRO, son of the said Juan and first wife, of Mosquitos, age 14
JUAN, son of the forementioned Juan and his second wife, of Mosquitos, age 6
GABRIEL, son of said Juan and second wife, of this [place], age 4
MARGARITA CASTELL, daughter of said Agueda and first husband, single, of Mosquitos, age 14

106.
ANTONIO MABRUMATI, farmer, of Milu [Milan?], age 35
FRANCISCA LLABRES, his wife, of Menorca, age 25
ANTONIO, son, of this [place], age 9
MARIA, daughter, of this [place] age 4
CATARINA LLABRES, daughter, of this [place], age 1
1 male Negro slave, not baptized

[s.1-199]

107.
BERNARDO ARNAU, farmer, of Menorca, age 36
MARIA SANS, his wife, of Menorca, age 28
PEDRO LLAMBRIS, son of Maria and first husband, of this [place], age 5

108.
LAZARO HORTEGAS, farmer, of Menorca, age 30
CATARINA LLABRES, his wife, of Menorca, age 25
CATARINA, daughter, of this [place], age 5
FRANCISCA, daughter, of this [place], age 1

[s.2-199]

109.
BARTOLOMEO ALCINA, farmer, of Menorca, age 46
MARIA, his wife, of Menorca, age 38

110.
MIGUEL GRACIAS, farmer, of Menorca, age 30
ANTONIA ESPINETA, his wife, of Menorca, age 27
MIGUEL GRACIAS, son, of this [place], age 2
MARGARITA, daughter, of this [place] age 6 months

111.
PEDRO MESTRE, farmer, of Menorca, age 38
MARIA ANOREU, his wife, of Menorca, age 30
JUAN, son, of this [place], age 6

1786: St. Augustine and Its Perimeter

[s.1-200]

111. (cont'd)
ANGELA [MESTRE], daughter, of this [place], age 4
MARIA, daughter, of this [place], age 11 months

112.
TOMAS ANDREU, farmer, of Menorca, age 26
MARGARITA PRETOS, his wife, of Menorca, age 22
JUAN, son of said Tomas and first wife, of this [place], age 5
FRANCISCA, daughter of said couple, of this [city], age 1

113.
JUAN ANDREU, farmer, of Menorca, age 42
CATARINA PONS, his wife, of Menorca, age 43
JUAN, son, of Mosquitos, age 16
MIGUEL, son, of Mosquitos, single, age 13
ANTONIO, son, of Mosquitos, age 10
FRANCISCA, daughter, of this [place], age 7

[s.2-200]

114.
DOMINGO SEGUI, farmer, of Menorca, age 23
MARGARITA SEGUI, his wife, of Menorca, age 26
DOMINGO SEGUI, son, of this [city], age 3

Totals:

Married couples of this Register	97
White Males	241
White Females	228
Male Negroes	33
Female Negroes	37
Total	539

1786: St. Augustine and Its Perimeter

Floridians

1.
SEVASTIAN ESPINOSA, single, mariner, of this [place], age 40
JOSEFA ESPINOSA, of this city, age 40
NICOLAS SANCHEZ, nephew, single, farmer, age 26
BERNANDINO SANCHEZ, nephew, single, shopkeeper, age 24
JOSEPH SANCHEZ, nephew, of this [place], farmer, age 22
RAMON SANCHEZ, nephew, native of Havana, mariner, age 18
MARIA DE LA O. SANCHEZ, niece, of Havana, single, age 20
MARIA ANDRES SANCHEZ, niece, of Havana, single, age 16
MARIA, daughter, of this [place], age 2
     5 male & 1 female negro slaves, baptized

[s.1-201]

2.
ALFONZO RIVERO, of this [place], tobacco merchant, age 30

3.
MIGUEL CHAPUS, of this [place], mariner, age 44
GETRUDIS CARRILLO, his wife, of this [place], age 33
JOSEPH JILLAN, son, of Havana, age 13
FRAN^{co} NAVARRO, mariner, lives with them, of this [place], age 35
JUANA PEREZ, free *morena*, of this [place], Catholic, age 54

[s.2-201]

4.
ANTONIO MONTES DE OCA, shoemaker, of this [place], age 47
PAULA DE TORES, his wife, of Menorca, age 39
MATEO LORENZO, son of Paula and first husband, of Mosquitos, single, crippled, age 16
JUANA LORENZO, son of Paula and first husband, of Mosquitos, age 11

5.
CATARINA AGUILAR, free Negress, married with her husband absent, Catholic, of this [place], age 48
JOSEPH A. RIVAS, free mulatto, of Havana, shoemaker, married, age 19

[s.1-202]

6.
LORENZO LLANES, mariner, single, of this [place], age 38
    one free mulatto, of this city
    one negro slave, not baptized

―――――――――― 1786: St. Augustine and Its Perimeter

7.
ANTONIO PUELLO, mariner, widower, of this [place], age 56
MARIA MANUELA, daughter, single, of this [place], age 14
ANTONIO, son, of Havana, age 12
    1 female negro slave, convert

8.
D^N FRAN^{CO} JOSEPH HUET, of this [place], merchant, age 30
D^A ROSALIA FAUSTINA, his wife, of Havana, age 33
ROSALIA, daughter, of Havana, age 10
MARIA NICOLASA, daughter, of Havana, age 7
JOSEPH RAMON, son, of Havana, age 3
MARIA DE LA CONCEPCION, daughter, of Havana, age 2
FRAN^{CO} JOSEPH, son, of Havana, age 1
                                                          [p.2–202]
D^N FRAN^{CO} HUET, father of said Dⁿ Fran^{co}, of Spain, third brother of
    Sⁿ FRAN^{CO}, lives with him, 78
LUIS CONTRERAS, single, of this [place], trader, lives with them, age 21
MARIA RITA BRAVA, single, of Havana, lives with him, age 17

9.
LORENZO RODRIGUES, of this [place], mariner, age 55
ISABELA PUIMA, wife, of Germany, Catholic, age 40
MARIA DEL CARMEN, daughter, of Havana, single, age 22
NICOLAS, son, mariner, single, of this [city], age 25 [sic]
THERESA DE JESUS RODRIGUES, daughter, of Havana, age 10
JOSEPH GONZALES, of Havana, single, lives with them, age 14
RICARDO BUSTAN, of America, single, lives with them, age 13
    1 free male *pardo* & 1 unbaptized female negro slave
                                                         [s.1–203]

10.
D^N THOMAS CORDERO, of this [place], merchant, age 63
D^A LEONOR GONZALES, of this [place], his wife, age 61
D^N IPOLITO GONZALES, notary public and native of this [place],
    widower, age 45
JUAN JOSEPH, son of said Dⁿ Ipolito, of Havana, age 14
JUANA DE DIOS, daughter of said Dⁿ Ipolito, of Havana, age 12

11.
JUANA MONTES DE OCA, widow, of this [place], age 44
JUAN EUGENIO GONZALES, son, single, of Havanna, age 17
JOSEPH, son, of Havana, age 10
ANTONIO JOSEPH, son, of Havana, age 5
LEONARDA JOSEFA, daughter, of Havana, age 2

1786: St. Augustine and Its Perimeter

12.
LUCIA ESCALONA, widow, of this [place], age 60
   1 male negro slave, Christian
   1 female negro slave, Christian

[s.2-203]

13.
NICOLASA GOMEZ, widow, of this [place], age 67
   2 male negro slaves, Christians
   2 female negro slaves, Christians

14.
FRANCISCO SANCHEZ, planter, single, of this [place], age 40
   3 free male *pardos*, Catholics
   6 free female *pardas*, Catholics
   27 male negro slaves, baptized
   12 female negro slaves, baptized
   14 male and female slave children, baptized

Totals:

Married couples of this Register	6
White Males	29
White Females	21
Male Negro Slaves and Free	42
Female Negro Slaves and Free	40
Total	132

———————————— 1786: St. Augustine and Its Perimeter

Spaniards

1.

PEDRO DE CALA, of Spain, mariner, single, age 36
  1 male negro slave, baptized
  2 female negro slaves, converted

[s.1-204]

2.

ANTONIO ROSPAIN, of Catalonia, taverner, single, age 32
  1 male negro slave, Christian

3.

MANUEL DE BEN, of Spain, taverner, single, age 40

4.

JUAN ZUARES, of Canary Islands, farmer, age 40
JUANA MARTIN, his wife, of Canary Islands, age 40
BARTOLOMEO ZUARES, son, of Canary Islands, single, age 14
GREGORIO ZUARES, son, of Canary Islands, single, age 13
JOSEPH ZUARES, son, of Canary Islands, age 8

5.

JOSEPH ANTONIO CORUNA, of Canary Islands, farmer, age 35
MANUELA SANCHEZ, his wife, of Canary Islands, age 36
ANTONIO, son, single, farmer, of Canary Islands, age 16
LUCIA ANTONIA, daughter, of Canary Islands, age 9
MARIA REGLA, daughter, of Canary Islands, age 6

[s.2-204]

6.

MANUEL RODRIGUEZ, of Spain, farmer, age 30
CATARINA ZUARES, his wife, of Canary Islands, age 32
ANTONIA VEGA, daughter of said Catarina and first husband, of Canary Islands, age 10
LUCIA, daughter, of Canary Islands, age 2
JOAQUIN, son of said Catarina and first husband, of Canary Islands, age 6

1786: St. Augustine and Its Perimeter

7.
PEDRO DE ACOSTA, of Canary Islands, farmer, age 35
CICILIA DE ANTILES, his wife, of Canary Islands, age 35
JOSEPHA MARIA, daughter, of Canary Islands, age 5
MARIA DEL CARMEN, daughter, of Canary Islands, age 4
LUCIA, daughter, of Canary Islands, age 2

[s.1-205]

8.
D^N MIGUEL ISNARDI, of Spain, married, his wife absent, age 32
EDUARDO WANTOS, of this Province, of Protestant religion, single, dependent of D^n Miguel, age 19
— [page torn] male negro slaves, not baptized
— [page torn] female negro slaves, two converts

9.
JUAN LUAY, of Catalonia, taverner, single, age 28

10.
ANTONIO RIVERAS, of Catalonia, mariner and taverner, single, age 32

11.
PEDRO GARCIA, of Spain, taverner, single, age 29

12.
FRANCISCO BLAS, of Spain, carpenter, age 29
MARGARITA REDONDO, his wife, of Havana, age 27
JUAN MIGUEL, son, of this [place], age 6 months

[s.2-205]

13.
FRANCISCO ROCH, of Spain, tailor, age 28
MARGARITA BARNET, his wife, age 20
FRANCISCA, daughter, of Providence, age 2
　　　　1 Christian Indian, lives with them

14.
ANTONIO DE PALMA, of Spain, taverner, age 27
MARGARITA MACTAIL, [MACFAIL?], his wife, of this [place], age 19
JUANA, daughter, of this [place], age 1
IGNACIO ORTEGAS, of Menorca, widower, store clerk, lives with them, age 50

1786: St. Augustine and Its Perimeter

15.
JUAN AGUILAR, of Canary Islands, farmer, age 50
MELCHORA RAMOS, his wife, of Canary Islands, age 50
JUAN, their son, single, farmer, of Canary Islands, age 20
TOMAS, son, of Canary Islands, age 16
CATALINA, daughter, of Canary Islands, age 16
[s.1–206]
MANUEL ZUARES, native of Catalonia, lives with them, farmer, single, age 27

16.
PABLO CORANA, of Ceuta, barman, age 28
JUANA ESCALONA, his wife, of Havana
FRANCISCO, their son, of Havana, -- [page torn]
MARIA DOLORES, daughter, of this [place], age 10 montha
— [page torn] male negro slaves, not baptized
— [page torn] female slaves, not baptized

Totals:

Married Couples of this Register	10
White Males	27
White Females	19
Male Negro Slaves	8
Female Negro Slaves	4
Indians	1
Total	59

1787

Census of Householders in East Florida

Floridians and Cubans

Translator's note:
The sections of this census contain no date. In the upper left corner of each introductory page is pencilled *"1793?."* However, the preface to the microfilmed collection labels it *1787*. Internal evidence—e.g., a comparison of household data with the 1786 and labeled 1793 censuses—suggests 1787 is correct; and the year is commonly accepted by historians of the colonial borderlands.

[s.2–102]

ANTONIO MONTES DE OCA

Native of Florida; Catholic; has a [*page torn*] wife, one son, one daughter; occupation shoemaker; inhabits a wood house opposite the house of MRS. CLARKE; does not want land.

JUANA MONTES DE OCA

Presented by her son JUAN GONZALES; native of Florida; widow with three sons and one daughter; inhabits a hut on Hornwork Street on a lot [or piece of ground] of the king; farms about two acres of land and requests more; has three horses and one cow.

LORENZO IANES [LLANES]

Native of Florida; Catholic; single, has two sons, one present and the other in Charleston; has four houses with registered documentation, one situated on Prison Street and three on Hospital Street, one of them he inhabits; occupation [*illegible*]; has one slave, three horses; does not have land but wants to farm.

Source Location: Docs. No. 408 through 411.

1787 Census of Householders

[s.1-103]
Dⁿ Franᶜᵒ Josef Guet

Native of Florida; has a wife, two sons, and three daughters; living with him are his father, a niece, and a first cousin; occupation, merchant; has three horses; has a house he inhabits, as shown in the registry, next to the British church, and [page torn] a plot of ground of the king facing the same house; has a [word torn] coming from the barracks; wants more land.

Miguel Chapus

Native of old Florida; has a wife and one son; has a nephew living with him and also a free female Negro, also of this [place]; has a house without owning a plot that he inhabits on Barracks Street; occupation [word torn]; has no land but wants to farm; has four horses.

Migˡ Ipolito Gonzales

Native of this city; widower with one son and one daughter; profession, notary public; lives with his brother-in-law THOMAS CORDERO on Treasury;

[s.2-103]

wants land for his children.

Thomas Franᶜᵒ Cordero

Native of this city; has a wife; occupation, trader; inhabits a house on Treasury Alley; requests land.

Franᶜᵒ Xavʳ Sanchez

Native of Florida; Catholic; single with three sons and five daughters; occupation, farmer; has a store in his house (with plot) on St. Charles Street; also four others with plots, three of them on the aforementioned street, another (with plot) on St. Patrick's Alley that Dⁿ Manˡ Almansa presently inhabits, with English documents; has some one thousand acres of land in the San Diego [St. James] plains, with British documents, and some fifty[?] acres with permission of the governor along the St. Johns River [torn] one of them

[s.1-104]

CRISSIANO, son of the Havanan named CAYETANO; has living with him in the aforementioned San Diego plains one Englishman named ROBERTO ANDRES, his religion Protestant, married with one son and one daughter; has two slaves of his own; has likewise living with him a free mulatto female named BEATRIS; has from one hundred to one hundred and thirty horses and about three hundred head of cattle.

1787 Census of Householders

Dᴺ Manuel Solana

Native of Florida; has a wife and two sons; occupation, farmer; has seven slaves and seventy-six horses; has five houses along Hospital Street and inhabits one of them; works twenty acres of land and wants more.

Adefonso Josef Rivera

Native of this city; is single; employed in the country; lives in a rented house on Barracks Street.

[s.2–104]

Dᴬ Josefa Espinosa

Native of Florida; widow; lives with her four nephews and two nieces; has five slaves; inhabits a house of Dᴺ Franᶜᵒ Sanchez on the coast; requests land to farm.

Juan Josef del Toro

Native of Florida; single; occupation, shopkeeper; lives with the pilot Dᴺ Juaᵁᴺ Escalona.

Antonio Pueyo

Native of this city; widower, has three sons and one daughter; occupation, shopkeeper; has a shop on the coast; inhabits a house next to the barracks of the King; has one slave and three horses; does not want land.

_____ 1787 Census of Householders

Census of Spaniards

[s.2-106]

MIGUEL IZNARDY

Native of Andalusia; married in Spain; profession, merchant; wants to devote himself to farming; requests lands suitable to his means if an apportionment can be made to him; has in his shop a young lad, a white Floridian of English origin, called EDWARD WALTON; likewise six slaves of his own, and about three houses in this city registered with the government, one of them on St. Charles Street; has likewise two schooners and one sloop of his own, also registered.

Translator's note: The following entry was crossed out.

ANTONIO BERTA

Native of Geneva; Catholic; has a wife and two daughters; has one slave; occupation, shopkeeper; has two houses, one with a plot of ground that he inhabits (as is shown in the registry) situated in the corner of the alley that crosses St. Charles Street to the hornworks, and the other without a plot in the Greek village.

[s.1-107]

PEDRO DE CALA

Native of Sanlúcar de Barrameda; single; has an English Protestant female living with him and she wants to convert; has two slaves; has a house, without plot of ground, that he inhabits near the barracks; occupation, mariner, and is presently on the long-boat *de la Barra*.

JUAN ROGAYA

Native of the Kingdom of Catalonia; single, lives with a friend named ANTONIO OLIVERAS; has a shop of beverages and food in the house that he inhabits on St. Charles Street; occupation, shopkeeper and mariner.

ANTONIO PALMA

Native of Cadiz; has a wife and one daughter; occupation, trader; has a shop and billiard room; has four houses, two located on two adjoining plots and the other two likewise; he inhabits one of them on Hospital Street; has one negro living with him called VILLI [BILLY], and one white servant called IG[NACI]O ORTEGAS from Mahón; does not have land but wants to farm.

37

1787 Census of Householders

[s.2-107]

PEDRO RODRIG^z

Native of the Canary Islands; single; occupation, shopkeeper; has a beverage shop next to the fort in a house he owns and inhabits, without owning a plot; does not want land.

FRAN^co ROCH

Native of the kingdom of Catalonia; has a wife and one daughter; occupation, tailor; inhabits a rented house on Hospital Street; does not want land.

ANDRES BARRIOS

Native of Galicia; is single; occupation, mariner and is presently employed on the *Falna*.

PEDRO GARCIA

Native of Galicia; is single; occupation shopkeeper; has a store and house that he inhabits on Hospital Street, the property — [*illegible*]; does not want land.

[s.1-108]

JUAN ANTONIO PULLARES

Native of Galicia; single; is employed in the country; works about three acres of land and requests more; lives on Hornworks Street in a cottage made of wood.

SANTIAGO CUELLA

Native of Galicia; occupation, mariner; presently employed on the *Falna*; single.

LORENZO RODRIG^z

Native of this city; has a wife, one son, and two daughters; occupation, merchant; has a beverage shop; has one female slave; inhabits a house of the king on the Plaza; has another house, with registered documents, on Hornworks Street; living with him are one English boy and another [who is his] nephew, and a white servant lad; has a free mulatto who was formerly a slave and — [*illegible*]; has no land but requests it.

[s.2-108]

MANUEL DEVEN

Native of the Kingdom of Galicia; single; occupation *ni*— [*illegible*]; has a house on Barracks Street that he inhabits; requests land.

1787 Census of Householders

PABLO CORTINAS

Native of Ceuta [in Morocco]; Catholic; has a wife, one son, and one daughter; occupation, stonemason; lives with his father-in-law JOAQ^N ESCALONA; has three slaves and half of a schooner; requests lands.

GERONIMO ALBARES

Native of Austria [?]; single; occupation, shopkeeper, and has a shop near the barracks which he inhabits; has two slaves; requests lands.

LORENZO COLL

Native of Mallorca; single; occupation, mariner; presently has a schooner in partnership with JUAN RODRIG^Z; likewise has land in partnership with the aforementioned [ALBARES], both being residents of the *presidio*.

[s.1–109]

1787 Census of Householders

Census of Mahones

MATHIAS PONS   [s.2-110]

Native of Mahón; is married; Catholic; has one son and two daughters; his occupation, farmer; farms some three acres of land in front of the entrance way to the Hornworks; has one female slave; has one horse; has a house with a registered lot located on Hornworks Street.

DEMETRIO TEDULACHE

Native of the Island of Candia [Crete] in the Levante; Catholic; is married with three sons; occupation, mariner; has a schooner in partnership with one of his sons; inhabits his own house without a plot, at the end of Hornworks Street.

MARCOS ANDREU

Native of Mahón; Catholic; has a wife, two sons, and two daughters; occupation, mariner; wants to farm two acres of land; has a house and lot of his own from the time of the English [occupation], with necessary justification of his title; and another of wood, without a plot, is situated on the alley that crosses behind the house of Dᴬ HONORIA CLARKE, the fort, Carlota Street, and the hornworks; on it [there is] a beverage shop.

JOSEF BUCHANY   [s.1-111]

Native of Liorna, Italy; Catholic; married; has one son and one daughter; occupation, mariner on the *Falna*; has moreover a beverage shop; has a house that he inhabits on a plot of his own, as is shown in the registry, situated on the alley that crosses from the street of the fort to the hornworks and to the [property] of Dᴬ HONORIA CLARKE; also has a cabin, without plot, next to the sacred ground.

ANTONIO MABROMATY

Native of the Island of Milos in the Archipelago of Levante; Catholic; has a wife, one son, and two daughters; occupation, farmer; has about four acres of land that he farms near the *Lecho*,* and wants to work two more; has a cabin on the same land; has three horses and one Negro.

---

*The site here is uncertain.

1787 Census of Householders

Franco Bousa

Native of Mallorca; Catholic; has a wife and three sons, two present and one in Charleston; inhabits a rented house of Mr LESLIE on Hospital Street; has a married daughter in his house (husband PEDRO PASQUO, absent) who has one daughter.

[s.2-111]

Juan Chenovant

Native of Mallorca; Catholic; has a wife, two sons, and three daughters; occupation, farmer; has three acres of land which he farms opposite the *Lecho* and wants to farm more; has a house he inhabits, without plot of ground, fronting the entrance of the hornworks.

Franco Arnau

Native of Mahón; Catholic; has a wife, two sons, and two daughters; his occupation, mariner; has a schooner of his own; has a house, without plot of ground, which he inhabits near the entrance of the hornworks; has three acres of land that he farms next to the *Lecho* and requests more; has one female Negro.

[s.1-112]

Don Pedro Cosifacho

Native of Corcisa; Catholic; married; has four daughters; has four female slaves; has a clothing and beverage shop; inhabits a house of his own, dating from before the transfer of the province, as justified with authentic documents; farms from forty to fifty acres of land and requests more; the house is located on Hornworks Street; has a schooner of his own with Spanish registration.

Vinzt Larderec

Native of Provins in France; Catholic; single; lives with a companion named JOSEF TURDAY [FURDAY?], with whom he owns a schooner; lives on Carlota Street in a rented house, in which he has a shop[?]; occupation, mariner.

[s.2-112]

Sevastion Coll

Native of Menorca; Catholic; has a wife and two sons; inhabits a house of the King opposite the priest's house; his occupation, carpenter.

Nicolas Stefanopoly

Native of Menorca; Catholic; has a wife, one son and two daughters; occupation, carpenter; inhabits a house, without plot, near the English Church.

1787 Census of Householders

Lorenzo Capo

Native of Menorca; Catholic; widower, with one son and one daughter; occupation, sacristan; has land in two sections, one of one hundred and twenty acres and the other of fifty; has a house, without title, on a lot fronting on the fort, and another of the king fronting the treasury building.

[s. 1–113]

Juan Rolan

Native of Dauphine, France; Catholic; single; occupation, hatter; inhabits a rented house on St. Charles Street; wants to establish himself in the city.

Juan Solon

Native of Menorca; Catholic; has a wife, one son, and one daughter, his occupation, farmer; works about four acres of land that backs onto the house of the governor and wants to farm more; has a house that he inhabits on Prison Street, that he owns himself and has registered; has three slaves.

Andres Pasety

Native of the Kingdom of Naples; Catholic; has a wife and two [word missing]; hairdresser; has one slave; lives in a rented house next to the house of the priest, D^N THOMAS [HASSETT]; farms about seven acres of land and wants to work more.

[s.2–113]

Caspar Popee

Native of Smyrna, in the Levante; Catholic; has a wife; occupation, farmer; has two and a half acres of land and wants to farm more; lives in a house that he rents, as part of the same house of ROQ^E LEONARDY.

Juan Cabedo

Presents himself in place of his mother, who is a widow; native of Menorca; Catholic; has a wife; occupation, tailor; has an apprentice named FRAN^{CO} PUEYO; has a female slave; has a house with plot of ground, registered, that he inhabits opposite the treasury building.

Simon Esteves

Native of Mayuncia [Mainz?], in Germany; Catholic; has a wife, two sons, and two daughters; his occupation, cartwright; has a cottage, without plot, on St. Charles Street; has three acres of land that he farms and wants to work more; has a clothing store.

1787 Census of Householders

[s.1-114]

PEDRO STOPA

Native of the Province of France; Catholic; has a wife, [illegible] sons, and a daughter; inhabits a house without plot in the Greek village; has three acres and wants more.

RAFAEL GIMENRY

Native of Menorca; Catholic; has a wife and three daughters; occupation farmer and fisherman; has a house that he inhabits, without a lot, on Hornworks Street; has a slave, one horse, and one cow; farms five acres of land past the Point and wants to farm more.

FRAN^{co} TRIAY

Native of Menorca; Catholic; widower; lives with and presents himself for his mother, who is a widow; has a house with plot that he inhabits on Hornworks Street; has five slaves; occupation, farmer; has one horse and three head of cattle; farms eleven acres of land and wants to work more.

[s.2-114]

MIGUEL SEGUY

Native of Menorca; Catholic; has a wife, four daughters, and one son; occupation, carpenter; lives in a rented house on the alley that crosses from Fort Street to the hornworks; asks to work more land.

GABRIEL SEGUI

Native of Mahón; Catholic; has a wife and two sons; occupation carpenter; lives in his own wood house, without a plot, in the Greek village; has a niece living with him named ANTONIA TRIAY; asks to work land.

[s.1-115]

JUAN CHANOPOLY

Native of Romancia [Romania?], in Levante; Catholic; widower; has three slaves; has one horse; works five acres of land and wants to cultivate more; has his own house with plot, registered, and located next to the end of Hornworks Street; occupation, carpenter.

PASQUAL SANTE

Native of Naples; Catholic; has a wife, one son, and one daughter; occupation, mariner; inhabits a cabin next to the fort, without its own plot.

1787 Census of Householders

Bernado Arnau

Native of Menorca; Catholic; has a wife and one son; occupation, farmer; works about three acres of land and wants more; inhabits a cottage of wood on his land.

[s.2-115]

Juan Segui

Native of Menorca; Catholic; has a wife and two sons; occupation, farmer; has a cabin which he inhabits next to the sacred ground; works five acres.

Domingo Segui

Native of Menorca; Catholic; has a wife and one son; occupation, farmer; works six acres of land fronting the entrance of the hornworks, on which parcel he has a cottage that he inhabits; does not want to work more.

Barth.^l Figueray

Native of Menorca; Catholic; has a wife, two sons, and a daughter; occupation, farmer; has a cottage, without a plot, that he inhabits on St. Charles Street, next to the fort; works about four acres of land and wants more.

Pedro Fuixa

Native of Menorca; Catholic; has a wife and six sons; occupation, farmer; works about four acres of land on a parcel coming from the Gov^n Grant [*illegible*]; has a cabin that he inhabits and asks to work more land.

[s.1-116]

Miguel Villalonga

Native of Menorca; Catholic; has a wife and four daughters; occupation, farmer; lives in a hut of his own, without a plot, next to the Sacred Ground; works about five acres of land and requests more.

Diego Hernandez

Native of Menorca; Catholic; has a wife, two sons and one daughter; occupation, farmer; lives in a rented house on the coast; works about three acres of land and asks for more; has a cabin, without plot, in the Greek village.

Fran^{co} Ponz

Native of Menorca; Catholic; single; occupation, farmer and mariner; lives with MIGUEL FIGUERAS, with whom he works three acres of land in the Gov^n Grant, and requests more.

1787 Census of Householders

Antonio Canter

Native of Menorca; Catholic; has a wife, three sons, and one daughter; has two slaves, one absent, and one free Negro living with him; occupation, ship master and pilot of the Coast; has two houses, one in which he lives on St. Charles Street with a plot, and another without a plot next to the fort; wants to devote himself to farming; has one horse.

[s.2-116]

Nicolas Salada

His wife presents for him, as [he] is on a voyage; native of Slavonia; Catholic; has a wife, one son, and two daughters; occupation, mariner; has two houses with plots; lives in one that is registered in the governor's archives, situated on the alley that crosses from St. Charles Street to the hornworks; the other is located on the same alley, is rented, and has English documentation.

Juan Vila

Native of Menorca; Catholic; single; occupation, sailor of the *Falna*; lives in a house opposite the aforementioned Nicolas Solada.

[s.1-117]

Vizente Casaty [Casaly?]

Native of Menorca; Catholic; has a wife, one son, and one daughter; occupation, carpenter; has one female negro; has two houses adjoining the barracks and lives in one of them that is shown on the registry to be his property, and the other is located next to the same place; has two and one half acres of land and wants to work more.

Antonio Tudichy

Native of Liorna; Catholic; has a wife and no children; occupation, mariner; lives in a house without plot located on Hornworks Street and wants land.

Josef Hernandez

Native of Mahón; Catholic; has a wife, two sons, and three daughters; occupation, farmer and fisherman; has a house without plot that he inhabits in the Greek village; works about one and a half acres of land and wants to farm more.

[s.2-117]

Lorenzo Capella

Native of Menorca; Catholic; has a wife and one daughter; occupation, fisherman and farmer; has a house that he inhabits in the Greek village, without a plot; works about one and a half acres and wants to farm more.

1787 Census of Householders

Fran^{co} Marin

Native of Tarragona [Spain]; Catholic; has a wife, one son, two grandsons, and one granddaughter; occupation, shoemaker; lives in a house of FATHER O'REILLY, on Hospital Street; has one slave; works about seven acres of land.

Josef Cla

Native of Menorca; Catholic; has a wife and three sons; occupation, mariner, and is at the present on the *Falna*; has a house without a plot that he inhabits in the Greek village; wants to farm land.

[s.1–118]

Antonio Revi

Native of Menorca; Catholic; widower with one daughter; occupation, mariner; has a cabin without a plot of land that he inhabits in the Greek village; farms two acres of land and requests more.

Antonio Berta

Native of Geneva; Catholic; has a wife and two sons; has one female slave; occupation, shopkeeper; has two houses, one with plot of ground upon which he lives and for which he has registration in his own name, situated at the corner of the alley that crosses St. Charles Street to the hornworks, and the other without plot of ground in the Greek village.

[s.2–118]

Luis Sochis

Native of Liorna; Catholic; has a wife and six sons; occupation, mariner; presently employed on the *Falna*; has a house, without plot of ground, in which he lives in the Greek village; does not have land but wants to farm.

Roberto Roche

Native of Mahón; Catholic; has a wife, one son, and one daughter; has a house and plot of ground, registered, in which he lives in the Greek village.

Pablo Sabatier

Native of Mahón; Catholic; has a wife, one son and one daughter; has a young servant boy and his mother-in-law living with him; has one slave; occupation, farmer; has a house, without plot of ground, in which he lives in the Greek village; works about twenty acres of land and requests more.

———————————————— 1787 Census of Householders

ANTONIO AUSIMA

Native of Mahón; Catholic; has a wife, one son, and three daughters; has three slaves; has a house, without plot of ground, in which he lives next to the castle; works about thirty acres of land and wants to farm more.

[s.1-119]

PEDRO MESTRE

Native of Mahón; Catholic; has a wife, two sons, and two daughters; occupation, farmer; farms about six acres of land in the Governor's Grant, where he has a cottage in which he lives; wants to farm more.

THOMAS ANDREU

Native of Menorca; Catholic; has a wife, one son, and one daughter; works about seven acres of land in a parcel called the Governor's Grant in which place he has a cottage where he lives; wants to farm more.

PEPINO PEDRO DE BURGO

Native of Corsica; Catholic; single; has one boy from Mahón living with him, two slaves and four horses; has four houses, one with a plot of ground, three have their titles registered, and the other came from the English; works twelve acres of land and wants more; has seven horses [?] and more than four cows.

[s.2-119]

JOSEF CARRERAS

Native of Mahón; Catholic; has a wife, one son, and one daughter; occupation, farmer; has a house in which he lives with one brother; the house is registered and is situated at the entrance of the hornworks; wants to farm.

JUAN TRIAY

Native of Mahón; Catholic; has a wife and four sons; occupation, farmer; has one slave; works ten acres of land and wants more; lives in a cabin on Hornworks Street.

DIEGO CARRERAS

Native of Mahón; Catholic; single; occupation, porter; lives in his brother's house next to the parish curate; works about five acres and wants more; has one horse.

JUAN ANDREU

Native of Menorca; Catholic; has a wife, three sons, and one daughter; occupation farmer; works about fifty acres of land in the Governor's Grant, where he has a cabin; wants to farm more.

1787 Census of Householders

[s.1-120]

Juan Chaunico

Native of Mahón; Catholic; has a wife, one son, and one daughter; occupation, mariner; presently employed on the *de la Barra*; lives in a house of FATHER O'REILLY next to the British Church; works about five acres and requests more.

Barth.^L Ronfrin

Native of Menorca; Catholic; has a wife and two sons; occupation, mariner and farmer; has a house in which he lives, registered, on Hornworks Street; works about five acres of land and wants more.

Josef Pons

Native of Menorca; Catholic; has a wife and one daughter; occupation, farmer; works about thirty acres of land, formerly that of GOVERNOR MOULTRIE and desires more; has a house, without plot, next to the barracks; has living with him an Englishman JUAN TAYLOR, who has a cottage with plot of ground southwest of the barracks and is [willing] to convert; has five horses, two present and three lost.

[s.2-120]

Josef Pons de Triay

Native of Mencora; Catholic; has a wife and five sons; has a female slave; has two houses with their plots of land, one in which he lives on St. Charles Street and the other next to D.^A HONORIA CLARKE; wants to farm, and does farm together with the afore-mentioned [?] more than thirty acres; has living with him a Portuguese named ANTONIO LEDO; one of his sons has a house, with plot of ground, held under Spanish documents.

Pedro Triay

Native of Mahón; Catholic; single; lives with his mother and his uncle GABRIEL FRAN; lives in a house of the king north of the governor's house; wants more land; occupation, farmer.

[s.1-121]

Matheo Pelegrin

Native of Liorna; Catholic; has a wife, one son, and one daughter; occupation, farmer; works about three acres of land next to the Greek village [where], on his own place, he has a wooden cottage in which he lives.

_____ 1787 Census of Householders

JOSEF ROSSI

Native of Florence, Italy; Catholic; has a wife, two sons, and three daughters; has a house, without plot of ground, in which he lives on Barracks Street; occupation, farmer; works about six acres of land and wants more.

FRAN^{co} PALLISER

Native of Mahón; Catholic; has a wife, one son, and two daughters; occupation, carpenter; has one female slave; has a house and plot of land with English documents, in which he lives, on Hornworks Street; works about three acres and wants more.

[s.2-121]

FRAN^{co} VILLA

Native of Mahón; Catholic; occupation, farmer; has a cabin, without a plot, in which he lives in the Greek village; works about four acres of land; does not want to work more; has a lost horse.

D^N ROQUE LEONARDY

Native of Modena, in Italy; Catholic; has a wife, three sons, and two daughters; occupation, farmer; has one male slave; has four houses with plots of land on Medical Street and lives in one of them; has twelve horses; works about fifty acres and wants more; has a house and a shop in the city.

BARTH^L AUSINA

Native of Mahón; Catholic; has a wife and two daughters; has a cabin in which he lives next to the Greek village; occupation, farmer; works about ten acres of land and wants to work more.

[s.1-122]

LORENZO ORTEGAS

Native of Mahón; Catholic; has a wife and two daughters; has one horse present and two missing; works about eight acres on a plantation called the Governor's Grant, where he has a cabin in which he lives; wants more [land].

JAYME PRAIS

Native of Mahón; Catholic; has a wife and one son; has a cottage with a plot belonging to PEPINO, in which he lives, on Hornworks Street; the land that he works is in partnership with PEPINO, as he has shown.

1787 Census of Householders

Josef Entes
Native of Menorca; Catholic; has a wife without children; occupation, farmer; has a house of his own, with registered documents, that he inhabits on St. Charles Street; asks to work land.

Barth^L Llopis
Native of Mencora; Catholic; has a wife, two sons, and one daughter; has a cabin in which he lives, without plot, at the entrance of St. Charles Street; has one Negro; asks for land.

[s.2-122]

Ant° Llambias
Native of Menorca; Catholic; single; occupation, carpenter; lives with D^N Fran^co Marin; does not want land.

Antonio Andreu
Native of Menorca; Catholic; has a wife, one son, and two daughters; has living with him a boy named YIMA [YUNA?] QUANADA; occupation, ship carpenter; has a house, without plot, next to the fort; wants to work land.

Juan Triay
Native of Menorca; Catholic; has a wife and two daughters; occupation, farmer and fisherman; has a house in which he lives, without a plot, in the Greek village; works two acres of land and wants more.

Josef Arnau
Native of Menorca; Catholic; has a wife; occupation, farmer; has a hut in the Greek village without plot in which he lives; works about eight acres of land and wants more in the Governor's Grant.

[s.1-123]

Andres Capella
Native of Menorca; Catholic; single; occupation, farmer; works land with the aforementioned Josef Arnau and lives in the same house.

Mig^L Garcia
Native of Menorca; Catholic; has a wife, one son; and one daughter; occupation, farmer; works about six acres of land in the Governor's Grant and wants more in that place; has a cottage where he lives.

_____ 1787 Census of Householders

BARTH.ᴸ CINTAS

Native of Menorca; Catholic; single; has his mother with him; occupation, tailor; lives in a rented cottage on Barracks Street; does not want land.

[s.2–123]

JORJE ESTEFANOPLY

Native of the Ajaccio, in Corsica; Catholic; single; profession, overseer of the property of MISTRESS PEVET [PERRET?]; does not have land but wants it.

ANTONIO EUBERTY

Native of Menorca; Catholic; has a wife, two sons, and four daughters; occupation, farmer; lives in a cottage next to the beach; works about six acres of land in the Governor's Grant, where he has a cabin; works more than three acres fronting the entrance of the hornworks and requests more; has one horse.

ANTONY C. MESTRE

Native of Menorca; Catholic; widower; lives with his mother ANTONIA MESTRE; occupation, farmer; has a house in which he lives next to the barracks; has a shop; has one horse; works, in partnership with his brother, fifteen acres of land and wants more.

ANTONIO CANOVAS

Native of Mahón; Catholic; has a wife and one son; lives in a rented house on Hospital Street; has one horse; works about fifteen acres of land and wants more.

[s.1–124]

JUAN VILLALONGA

Native of Menorca; Catholic; has a wife and three daughters; has one female slave with two sons; has a house of his own with registered documents, on Hornworks Street; works about five acres of land and wants more.

MARTIN HERNANDES

Native of Menorca; Catholic; has a wife and two daughters; has a white apprentice and a female mulatto with one son; has two houses, one with a plot and the other is vacant; the one in which he lives has English documents; works several acres of land and wants more.

JUAN FRAN.ᶜᵒ ARNAU

Native of Marseilles, France; Catholic; has a wife and two daughters; occupation, mariner; inhabits a house in the city; has one horse; wants land.

1787 Census of Householders

[s.2-124]

Juan Carreras

Native of Menorca; Catholic; has a wife and one daughter; occupation, carpenter; lives in a cabin in the Greek village; does not have land but wants it.

Josef Gomila

Native of Menorca; Catholic; widower; occupation, carpenter; has one male negro; inhabits a house owned by his son-in-law, the master carpenter; has a house without a plot next to the fort and another with a plot on the main street.

Ferdnando Fatany

Native of Florence; has a wife, one son, and two daughters; occupation, farmer; has a cottage next to the barracks; works a parcel of land and wants more; lives on land adjoining Governor Moultrie.

[s.1-125]

Isabel Perpal

Native of Menorca; Catholic; is married, her husband absent; has two daughters and two sons; one daughter is married, her husband absent, and has one son; one of the sons is absent; has six slaves, two horses, and one cow; has two houses in this city on the Plaza and lives in one of them under Spanish documents; farms forty acres of land with a house near the large orange groves, considered to be the same land she owns by virtue of a deed passed

[s.2-125]

before his Excellency D^N DOMINGO RIDRIG^Z DE LEON by D^N JESSE FISH, on the understanding that the buyer is responsible to the King for any reclamation proceedings resulting from the seller, D^N JESSE FISH, not having presented a legal power of, much less documents of ownership from, the English owner D^N ELIAS BALL; under the same circumstances, she has some houses immediately to the north of the Governor's House also 500 acres of land, some 5 miles on the other side of the —*Iferia?*, under British documents, and requests more land; living with her are two Negroes called THOMAS and MARIA, who are free.

Josef Bataliny

Native of Menorca; Catholic; single; occupation, store clerk; lives with the Minorcan Priest.

Jaimio Pau

Native of Menorca; Catholic; single; occupation, mariner; presently employed on the *Herreria*; lives in a rented house on the plaza.

1787 Census of Householders

[s.1-126]

JUAN FERRI [TERRI?]

Native of Menorca; Catholic; has a wife who is absent; occupation, farmer; inhabits a cabin of his own, without a plot, in the alley that crosses St. Charles Street down to the hornworks.

JUAN CAPO

Native of Menorca; has a wife, three sons, and one [blank]; occupation, farmer; has two slaves and one male servant; works about twenty acres of land at GOVERNOR MOULTRIE's place, and wants more in his own place; has a cabin without plot next the fort; has one horse.

DIEGO SEGUI

Native of Menorca; has a wife and two daughters; occupation, mariner; inhabits a cabin, without its own plot, next to the fort; works about eight acres of land and wants more.

JUAN LORENS

Native of Mahón; has a wife, three sons, and two daughters; occupation, bricklayer; has a house that he inhabits next to the cemetery, without plot; does not have land but wants it.

[s.2-126]

BERNARDO SEGUI

Native of Menorca; has a wife, two sons, and four daughters; occupation, trader; has a supply store; has three houses, one that he inhabits on Hospital Street, the other on the alley of the said street, and the other on Barracks Street; works about thirteen acres of land behind the house of the governor, [for which he pays the tithe to the mayor of the city]; has three mares in *Monte Cerina* and one horse that has been stolen; has two female negroes and one small negro boy; wants more land to farm.

LUIS BUCHANTINY

Native of Liorna; Catholic; has a wife; occupation, ship's master[?]; inhabits a rented house in the city; does not want land.

JOSEF HERNANDEZ

Native of Mahón; Catholic; has a wife and one son; occupation, farmer; has a cottage, without plot, that he inhabits in the Greek village; works about four and a half acres of land and does not want more; has one horse.

1787 Census of Householders

[s.1–127]

Pedro Drimarach

Native of Corsica; widower with one son and one daughter; lives with JUAN CHANAPOLY; wants land; occupation, carpenter.

Domingo Seropoly

Native of Brazo de Magna [Mayna?], in Levante; has a wife; inhabits a house next to the fort; occupation, carpenter; wants land.

Josef Espineta

Native of Mahón; Catholic; has a wife and one son; occupation, mariner; has a cottage on a plot of the king next to the hornworks; has one acre of land.

Juan Pons

Native of Menorca; Catholic; has a wife, without children; occupation, fisherman; has a cottage in which he lives without plot, next to the Greek village; does not have land but wants it.

[s.2–127]

Isavel Moore

Native of Menorca; Catholic; presents for her absent husband; has two absent sons and two daughters who are present; occupation, seamstress; inhabits a rented house on the alley of St. Gerome; does not want land.

Margarita Capella

Native of Menorca; Catholic; has an absent husband; has one son and one daughter; has a house without a plot adjoining the hornworks, which she inhabits; does not want land.

Lucia Pedro de Borgo

Native of Menorca; Catholic; has one son; a widow; has two houses of wood, without plots, one in which she lives near the barracks; works about one acre of land and wants more.

[s.1–128]

Fran^{co} Mecholy

Native of Corsica; has a wife, two sons, and one daughter; occupation, mariner; does not have land nor does he want it; has a house, without plot, which he inhabits on Hospital Street.

1787 Census of Householders

Josefa Cassella

Native of Menorca; religion Catholic; presents for her absent husband ANGELO BAQUERY; has two sons and one daughter; has a cottage of wood on Barracks Street, but lives with D^N FRAN^CO GUETT.

Juana Hernandez

Native of Menorca; widow with one son; has a married daughter, who has a male child; occupation, seamstress; has a house, without a plot, in the Greek village which she inhabits; does not want land.

Juan Bautista [no surname]

Native of France; Catholic; single; occupation, blacksmith, and is presently employed in the King's smithy, where he lives.

Josef Bonely

[s.2–128]

Native of Italy; Catholic; has a wife and four sons; lives on a ranch of D^N FRAN^CO PH^E FATIO; has one female negro living with him; has four horses.

Pedro Stopa

Native of Mahón; Catholic; has a wife and one son; occupation, farmer; lives in a house of MR JOSE HUDSON at the north of Government Springs; works about three acres of land and requests more; has one horse.

Josef Cobachichosa

Native of Italy; Catholic; single; occupation, mariner; does not have a house; lives with JOSEF FURDAS [TURDAS?] and does not request land.

1787 Census of Householders

Census of British Residents

[s.2–130]

Don Fran^{co} Ph^e Favio

Native of the Canary Islands; Catholic; profession, merchant and planter; has 17,824 acres in different parcels within the province held under American documents that he can present when necessary; is married, with one son and one daughter [present], and two sons and one daughter absent; also has in his house D^N JORJE HERRISON, native of Ireland and Catholic, as is D^A JUANA CROSS, who is Irish Catholic, and an orphan; has in this place three houses which he owns under Spanish registration; he inhabits one of them on the coast, the other is being used by him now as a warehouse for his goods; has eighty slaves; has more than one hundred head of cattle and twenty or more riding horses [*page torn*] and breeders; is the owner of a schooner and a sloop, the first is not registered, the second is.

Tophilo Hill

Native of South Carolina; Protestant, but wants to convert himself and his family to the Catholic religion; has a wife and four daughters; profession, farmer; has eleven slaves and farms some fifty acres of land eight miles above North River; lives with his family in the house next to DIEGO MACGIRT until he is able to build a house of his own; wants to work more land.

[s.1–131]

Diego Clark

Native of Scotland; Protestant; profession, trader and innkeeper; married, without children; he has taken charge of a white orphan boy, who has neither father nor mother, about thirteen years of age, named DIEGO TATE; has one female negro that belongs to him and another living with him whom is said to be free, but was the property of a Britisher who left the province; has his own house, with British documents, on Hornworks Street, which he inhabits; has a coffee house on St. Charles Street.

Jorje Backhayse

Native of the East Indies; Protestant, but is soon to convert to the Catholic religion; occupation, tailor and surgeon [?]; lives in a house, without paying rent, next to [?]; has one slave.

_____ 1787 Census of Householders

[s.2-131]
Dᴬ HONORIA CLARKE

Native of Ireland; Catholic; widow with four sons and two daughters, one of each sex was sent away before the transfer of the province by His Majesty; profession, farmer; has two thousand five hundred acres of land in several different places in the province, held under British documents—as likewise three houses and plots in this city, one she inhabits on St. Charles Street, another adjoining the treasury building, and the other near the barracks; has fifteen slaves and one free person living with her; has likewise three head of cattle and four horses.

DANIEL GRIFFIN HOWARD

Native of Ireland; Catholic; single; called to this province by his uncle[?] Captain Dᴺ CARLOS HOWARD, with the intention of dedicating himself to farming; is a lodger in the house of Dᴬ HONORIA CLARKE.

[s.1-132]

ISAVEL BOYCE

Native of Georgia; Protestant; widow with one son; profession, seamstress; her mother, a widow, lives with her, also a sister [?] named MARIA, and another widow named REGINA MARGARITA MEYERHOVEN; has her own plot of ground held under authentic British documents, and inhabits a rented house on Hospital Street.

JUAN HOPKINS

Native of England; Protestant; has a wife; occupation, shoemaker; lives with an officer [?] named GROVES DORAN, Irish Catholic, and a Minorcan boy apprentice; has a house that he inhabits [*illegible*] within the Greek village by permission of the interim government.

[s.2-132]
EDUARDO ASHTON

Native of Ireland; Catholic; has a wife, four sons, and three daughters, one of these absent; occupation, tailor; farms one hundred acres of land above North River in partnership with his son-in-law [stepson] JUAN PARISH; he lives (thanks to the graciousness of the deceased MR. PEABET) in a house on St. Charles Street.

1787 Census of Householders

Juan Leslie

Native of Scotland; Anglican; profession, merchant in Indian goods; has living with him in his warehouse in this city a white caretaker in charge of goods named D^N Juan Foraster, Scottish, and also Anglican; and an apprentice Josef Clarke, Floridian and Catholic; has four male slaves and seven female slaves; has a house, with plot, where he has his warehouse, and another plot and house on Hospital Street; inhabits a house belonging to the king above the bay; in his Saint John's warehouse there resides another caretaker of his called White[?].

[s.1-133]

D^N Juan Hambley

Native of England; Anglican; has a wife, two sons, and two daughters; resides in the same warehouse.

D^N Jayme Leslie

Native of America; has a wife; is in charge of more than two hundred head of cattle and some twelve horses that are the property of the informant and the company of which he is a partner; in the same warehouse, and belonging to the same business, are twenty five slaves; also belonging to D^N Juan Leslie and Company are 7,420 acres of land in different places of the Province, held under authentic British documents.

Thomas Cordero

Native of Pennsylvania; Protestant; has a wife and one son with him and three away, one in Louisiana; has likewise with him a grandson and an Englishwoman Cataline Morain, placed [there] by the Court; inhabits a house with a plot next to the old English Church, by permission of the governor; occupation, butcher; has a mule; does not have land but wants to farm.

[s.2-133]

Barbara Simpson

Native of Pennsylvania; Catholic; widow with one son and one daughter; supports herself by sewing and washing; inhabits a house of the governor's brother, in satisfaction of [illegible]; wants a bit of ground in the country whenever there is a place to have.

Antonio Heinsman

Native of Pennsylvania; Catholic; has a wife, and a son; occupation, farmer; farms seven or eight acres but needs to farm more; lives above the North River; has four horses and a lot by permission of the governor on Hornworks Street.

1787 Census of Householders

[s.1-134]

ALEXANDRO MACDONALD

Native of Scotland; Catholic; single; occupation, farmer; farms with permission of the governor — [?] acres of land in partnership with RUDULFO MACDONALD above North River, where he has a cabin; they both live in a rented house, property of MANUEL SOLANA, adjoining the house of the same Manuel; between them, they have six slaves and three horses, and requests land proportionate to the slaves that they have.

DUNCAN NOBLE

Native of Scotland; Catholic; single; occupation, tailor; lives with the aforenamed MCDONALD.

JUAN JORJE HEINSMAN

Native of Maryland; Catholic; has a wife without children; occupation, farmer; has thirteen horses; has a house of his own with plot on Treasury Street, held by British documents; lives in the country above North River where he farms fifteen acres of land and wants to farm more.

[s.2-134]

DON JESSE JUSTI[?]

Native of New York; Protestant; is married, with a wife and two sons away; profession, farmer; has seventeen slaves and, without counting, hundreds of horses on the Island of St. Anastasia Cimarones.

[s.1-135]

D^N THOMAS FONNO

British *Horallo* [?] with the intention of returning as soon as he collects the several sums that are owed him by the government, and particularly [those owned to] the Spanish or British retirees who have given him their power of attorney, which debts ought to be satisfied in conformity to the terms of the peace treaty.

FRAN^{co} HONIT

Native of North Carolina; Protestant, but wants to convert; has a wife, two sons, and three daughters [*written as* sons]; is occupied in farming land but is by occupation a chairmaker; farms more than eighteen acres of land above the Tertianta [?] Spring; has fourteen farm horses on St. Johns River.

1787 Census of Householders

BARBARA HEINSMAN

Native of L'Orient in France; Catholic; widow; has four married daughters with her [*illegible words*]; has some single daughters also; lives in a house with a married son on Treasury Alley; has two hundred acres of land above the Spring of North River held under authenic British documents; has two horses.

[s.2-135]

D^N JUAN HUDSON

Native of Ireland; Catholic; has a wife and a white boy living with him; has forty-six slaves, seventeen horses and six cows; has five houses with English documentation and one of Spanish, the one that he inhabits adjoins the barracks, another adjoins the treasury building, two adjoin St. Charles Street, and another lies to the north of the governor's house; has, by documents, [*blank*] acres of land and requests more; has another house above the same land.

[s.1-136]

D^N MIG^L O'REILLY

Native of Ireland; Catholic; married with three sons in his household; occupation, merchant; lives in a house of LIEUTENANT ARNAU.

[s.2-136]

Talbot Island

SPICER CHRISTOPHER

Native of Georgia; Protestant; occupation, farmer; has a wife and one daughter; has seven slaves and two free persons living with him; has seven horses and is a partner in a sloop; farms some thirty acres of land, is able to farm more and requests more.

TIMOTEO HOLLINGSWORTH

Native of North Carolina; Protestant; is married with two sons and four daughters; occupation, farmer; has nine slaves, and one white servant and a Negro renter; farms fourteen acres of land, is able to and wants to farm more.

1787 Census of Householders

GUILLERMO HENDRICKS

Native of North Carolina; Protestant; is married; has two sons and two daughters; his occupation, farmer and millwright; has three Negroes and one white servant; has one horse and half of a sloop with twenty-five feet of keel; farms some twenty acres of land and is able to farm much more.

[s.1-137]

GUILLERMO BALENTINE

Native of Georgia; Protestant; is married; farms some ten acres of land and is able to farm some more.

ROBERTO WHITMORE

Native of England; Protestant; is married; has one daughter; his occupation, farmer; farms some ten acres of land and wants to farm more.

GUILLERMO SIMPSON

Native of England; Protestant; is a widower with two sons; occupation, carpenter and farmer; farms some ten acres of land and wants more.

St. George's Island

JOSEPH SABY

Native of Italy; Catholic; married; has a son; has two white male servants and an orphan girl living with him; is owner of a small sloop; requests land.

Amelia Island

[s.2-137]

MARIA MATEOR

Native of Virginia; Protestant; widow with one son and one daughter; profession farmer and laundress; has three horses and farms some five acres of land.

1787 Census of Householders

Jorje Arons

Native of France; Catholic; is married; has one son; has living with him a widow named ROSA EAGER, with one son; has ten male negroes and seven horses; farms some twenty-five acres of land, with authority to farm more.

Juan Loftin, Sr.

Native of Virginia; is a widower with one son and one daughter; Protestant; occupation, farming; has two female slaves, one horse, and fifteen head of cattle; farms some twenty acres of land and is able to farm much more.

Juan Loftin, Jr.

Native of North Carolina; Protestant; single; occupation, farmer; has two negroes, one horse and nineteen head of cattle; farms ten acres of land and is able to farm much more.

[s.1–138]

Guillermo Bogin

Native of South Carolina; Protestant; is married; has one daughter; his occupation, farmer; has two negroes; farms ten acres of land and requests more.

Pedro Jennings

Native of Virginia; Protestant; married; has two sons and four daughters; his occupation, farmer; has five horses and eight head of cattle; farms ten acres of land and requests more.

Juan Hartley

Native of South Carolina; Presbyterian; is married; has three sons; his occupation, farmer; has one negro, three horses and fourteen head of cattle; farms ten acres and requests more.

Juan Bailie

Native of Maryland; Protestant; married; has two sons and one daughter; occupation, farmer; has four slaves, eight horses and twenty head of cattle; farms some fifteen acres of land; is able to farm more and requests more; has living with him the wife of the overseer of D^N GUILLERMO PENOGREE.

_____ 1787 Census of Householders

[s.2-138]

JOSEF RAINS

Native of Maryland; Protestant; is married; has three sons and two daughters; occupation, farmer; has six negroes, eight horses, and seventy head of cattle; farms eighteen acres of land; is able to farm more and requests more.

FREDERICO HARTLEY

Native of North Carolina; Protestant; is married; has one son and one daughter; occupation, farmer; has one horse and three head of cattle; farms some five acres of land and requests more.

JUAN DOGHARTY

Native of Virginia; Protestant; is married; occupation, blacksmith; has one male negro; one horse and twelve head of cattle; living with him, without family, is WIDOW JOHNSON; farms some twelve acres of land and requests more.

[s.1-139]

THOMAS SIMS

Native of North Carolina; Protestant; is married with two sons; occupation, farmer; has two horses and twenty head of cattle; farms some five acres and requests more.

ENRIQ^E O'NEIL

Native of Virginia; son of Catholic parents but was raised as a Protestant orphan; is married, with seven sons and one daughter; occupation, farmer; has one white male servant and one white female servant living with him; has nineteen horses; farms thirty-five acres of land and three hundred that he holds under British documents.

RUBEN HODGINS

Native of Virginia; Protestant; is married, with two sons and four daughters; occupation, farmer; has six negroes, two horses, and eight head of cattle; has some five acres of land and requests [more].

[s.2-139]

CORNELIO GRIFFITHS

Native of South Carolina; Protestant; married; has two daughters; occupation, joiner; has three horses, sixteen head of cattle; farms some five acres of land and requests more.

1787 Census of Householders

Juan Houston

Native of Georgia; Protestant; married; has three daughters; occupation, farmer; has twenty-two slaves, one horse, and six head of cattle; lives with his mother-in-law, a widow; farms some twelve acres of land and requests more.

Guillermo Kean

Native of Pennsylvania; Catholic; is married, with two sons and three daughters; occupation, farmer; has one Negro, three horses, and eight head of cattle; lives with his brother; farms some twenty acres of land and requests more.

[s.1–140]

Sarah Hall

Native of South Carolina; Protestant; widow; two sons; occupation, farmer; has two negroes, two houses, and two head of cattle; farms twenty-five acres of land.

Ricardo Lang

Native of South Carolina; Protestant; is married, with two sons and four daughters; occupation, farmer; has one negro, two horses, and eleven head of cattle; is owner of a sloop with twenty-two feet of keel; requests land.

Josef Sumerland

Native of South Carolina; Protestant; married, with one son and one daughter; occupation, farmer; has three horses and six head of cattle; requests land.

[s.2–140]

Daniel Hoggins

Native of Georgia; Protestant; has one son and one daughter; occupation, farmer, has three horses and thirteen head of cattle.

St. Johns River

D^N Luis Fatio

Native of Nice in the Piedmont [of Italy]; Catholic; married; has one daughter; lives and farms the hacienda of his father FRAN^{co}, under the overseer RICARDO GUSCAIN, a Protestant Englishman, single, as well as GUILLERMO CAPMAN, foreman; and GASPAR BARTER, another foreman, an American Protestant widower with absent sons; the above-mentioned Luis has a house in this city.

_____ 1787 Census of Householders

DIEGO CLOTWORTHY
Native of England; Protestant; married, with one son; is also a foreman on the ranch of FATIO.

ROEFULFO TOMPSON
Native of England; Protestant; occupation, carpenter; farms six acres of land and requests more.

[s.1-141]

THOMAS COLSTON
Native of England; Protestant; married, and has two absent [blank]; occupation, farmer; has four slaves and two horses; farms some twelve acres of land and requests more.

ANAH MOORE
Native of America; Protestant; widow, with one son; occupation, farmer; has nine slaves and six horses; farms some forty acres of land and requests more; living with her is her forman JUAN GRAY, free mulatto, who has two horses, two head of cattle, and one free negro male living with him.

ANGUS CLARK
Native of Scotland; widower; Protestant; has one daughter present and another absent; occupation, farmer; has six negroes, four head of cattle, and twenty-six horses; farms some forty acres of land and requests more; living with him is the widow ISABEL HOLMES, with three American Protestant sons.

[s.2-141]

ISACH RIOAS
Native of the Swiss Cantones; Protestant; is married, but his wife and children are absent; occupation, watchmaker; has a ranch that is said to be his own property, called Mesoptamia, of 4,000 acres.

FRAN^{co} HORIT [FLORIT?]
[Name and entry crossed out.]

ISACH BURDEN, JR.
American Protestant; married, with two sons; occupation, farmer; has one cow; farms some eight acres of land and requests more.

1787 Census of Householders

Jesse Frost

Native of America; Protestant; single; farmer; farms some six acres.

Guillermo Pengree

Native of England; Protestant; married; has two stepchildren; occupation, farmer; has fifty-three negroes, one hundred head of cattle, and five horses; living with his family is the overseer ROBERTO COWEN, and one sister, both American Protestants; also ROBERTO PRITCHARD, American Protestant, married with one son and three slaves; also DANIEL PLOMER, American Protestant, single, with five negroes; D^n Guillermo requests land proportionate to his family.

[s.1-142]

Ricardo Malpas

American Protestant; married, with two sons; has three head of cattle, farms some six acres and requests more.

Issack Bowden

American Protestant; single; has one horse and farms some six acres of land

Samuel Eastlake

American Protestant; married; profession, doctor [?] and farmer; has two slaves and three houses; farms some fifteen acres of land and requests more.

[s.2-142]

Isack Bowden, Sr.

American Protestant; married and has two sons; farms twenty acres of land and requests more.

Guillermo, Jayme, and Aaron Travies, brothers

American Protestants; all single, they live with a widowed sister, who has one son; they request land.

Salomon King

American Protestant, married; has three sons; occupation, farmer; has nine slaves.

Josef Swald

American Protestant; married with two sons; occupation, carpenter; requests land; has living with him one negro, with a wife and two sons.

1787 Census of Householders

AMBROSIO NELSON
American Protestant; married; has two sons; occupation, carpenter; requests lands; has living with him one negro, with a wife and two sons.

ROBERT WHITMORE
[*His entry crossed out.*]

[s.1-143]

GUILLERMO BALENTINE
[*No information given.*]

JOSEF MACCULLOCK
Native of Florida; Protestant; married; has one son; occupation, farmer; has five horses and fifteen head of cattle; has likewise one mulatto, and farms twenty acres of land.

JONATAN MACCULLOCK
Native of Florida; Protestant; married, has one son; occupation, farmer; lives with his brother, the before-named, and both request land.

SAMUEL WILSON
American Protestant; married; occupation, farmer; has one horse and one cow; farms twelve acres of land and requests more.

[s.2-143]

PEDRO LANE
American Protestant; single; occupation, farmer; has two slaves, one horse, and two cows; farms twelve acres of land and requests more.

JOSEF BONELY
[*His name is crossed out.*]

GUILLERMO LANE
American Protestant; married and has five sons; has three slaves, six horses, and seven head of cattle; farms some eighteen acres of land and requests more.

JUAN CONWAY LADSON
American Protestant; married; farms some eight acres.

1787 Census of Householders

Josef Mills

American Protestant; married; has two slaves, six horses, and seven head of cattle; farms some eighteen acres and requests more.

Thomas Pemberton

Native of England; Catholic; single; resides five miles from the head of St. Johns River; has one brother named JORJE, absent (with the permission of the governor) in Charleston.

Manuel Marzail

Native of Ma—a—; married; has one son; has one female negro; lives two leagues from the ford of the St. John's [River]; requests lands.

Jesse Youngblood

American Protestant; single; was a sailor on the *Falna de Sta. Maria*; farms.

Diego MacGirtt

American Protestant; wants to convert with his family; is married, with five sons and one daughter; occupation, farmer; has six slaves and six horses; farms forty acres of land and requests more.

Josef Hughes

Native of England; Protestant; widower, with one son; bricklayer and farmer; has two horses; living with him are two white associates, one called JESSE ESTHERS[?], and the other LUIS, both Americans; inhabits and farms some ten acres of land above the Matanzas River, opposite the detachment.

Dionisio [no surname]

Native of Ireland; Catholic; single; occupation barber.

1793

St. Augustine and North River

Street of the Coast from the Barracks to the Fort

[s.2-145]

1.
New Barracks [*no individuals named*]

2.
MARIA ANA ROQUERA, daughter of Santiago and of Isabel Arnau, age 56, married to Josef Ponz, absent

3.
GERONIMO ALVAREZ, son of Mig[l] and of Theresa Alvarez, age 34
ANT[A] VENZ, his wife, daughter of Guillermo and of Maria Ana Roquera, age 20
TERESA MARIA ANT[A], their daughter, age 4
ANT[O] JOSEF, their son, age 2
                2 male slaves not baptized

4.
CECILIA JULIANA, free negress, age 62, widow
JUAN BAUTISTA COLLINS, free mulatto, her son, single, age 29
MARIA ROSA ANA, daughter of said Juan, age 3

5.
Vacant house

Source location: sheets 1–145 through 1–166.

1793: St. Augustine and North River

6.

JUAN BILOT, JR., son of Juan and of Rebecca Crandel, married, age 32, Protestant
ABIGAIL BILOT, his wife, Protestant, age 25
ISABEL, free negress, age 45, not baptized
FIBY, free negress, baptized, living with them [no age given]
GEORGE, son of the before-said Juan, age 8
MIG^L, age 4, not baptized

7.

D^A JOSEFA ESPINOSA, daughter of Diego and of Josefa Torres, widow, age 51
SEBASTIAN ESPINOSA, her brother, single, age 4 [sic], single
NICOLAS SANCHEZ, son of Josef and of Ant^a Espinosa, age 32, single
    JOSEF SANCHEZ, brother of Nicolas, age 29
RAMON SANCHEZ, his brother, age 25
D$^{[n]}$ VICENTE LLERENA, son of D$^{[n]}$ Josef and of D^a Maria del Carmen Hernandez, age 29
D^a MARIA DE LA O. SANCHEZ, his wife, daughter of Josef and of Ant^a Espinosa, age 26

[s.1-146]

MARIA TERESA LLERENA, their daughter, age 4
RITA MARIA, her sister, age 2
JUAN NEPOMUCENO VIDAL, brother, age 1 month
DAMASO, negro slave of Josefa Espinosa, age 20
CRESPIN, negro slave of same, age 17
HENRIQUE, mulatto slave of same, age 14
MARIA DEL PILAR, free mulatto, age 3, parents unknown
MARIA, female slave of the same, age 26, not baptized
MANUELA, female slave of Josefa Espinosa, age 14, not baptized

8.

Vacant house

9.

LUIS CAPELLA, son of Jose and of Ana Veri [?], age 40
MARGARITA ROQUER, his wife, daughter of Juan and of Margarita Arnau, age 44
ANA, their daughter, single, age 18
FRAN^{co}, their son, single, age 13

10.

CATALINA PONZ, free negress, age 43
CATALINA BROWN, free *parda*, married to Juan Ant^o Garcia, Indian, living with her, age 18
MAGDALENA GARCIA, daughter of said [Catalina Brown], age 1

1793: St. Augustine and North River

11.
FRAN^{co} MARIN, son of Ant° and of Tecla Casalo, age 68
MAGDALENA ESCUDERO, his wife, daughter of Ant° and of Juana Mir, age 52 [55?]
FRAN^{co} MARIN, their son, single, age 22
GORJE MEDOCHI, son of Elias and Tecla Marin, single, age 19, living with them
FRAN^{co}, his brother, age 22
ANT°, male slave, not baptized, [*no age given*]
MAGDALENA JOANEDA, daughter of Juan and of Mag^{la} Marin, single, age 10, living with them

12.
Barracks

13.
JOSEF ROSI, son of Pedro and of Marga^{ta} Salti, age 52
FRAN^{ca} SANZ, his wife, daughter of Gaspar and of Angela Hernandez, age 35

[s.2–146]

FRAN^{ca}, their daughter, age 14
GASPAR, their son, age 9
JOSEF, his brother, age 7
CATALINA, his sister, age 3

14.
BARTOLOMEO CINTAS, son of Bineto and of Magdalena Cintas, age 29
ANT^a REU, his wife, daughter of Alonso and of Margar^{ta} Alcina, age 18
MAGDALINA CINTAS, daughter of Bartolomeo and of Juana Juvera, widow, age 56

15.
MIG^L CHAPUZ, son of Josef and of Beatrix Amadona, age 46
GETRUDIZ CARILLO, his wife, daughter of Fran^{co} and of Fran^{ca} Rodrig^z, age 37
JOSEF JULIAN CHAPUZ, their son, single, age 21
JUANA PEREZ DE LA ROSA, free negress, age 84, widow

16.
D^N JUAN JOSEF BUSQUET, son of Josef and of D^a Sebastiana de Fuentes, age 40
D^A MARIA JOSEFA BLAN[co], his wife, daughter of Dⁿ Josef and of Maria Ant^a Mans, age 36
JOSEF MARIA, their son, age 13
AGUSTINA MARIA, his sister, age 11
JOSEF GABRIEL, male slave, age 15
D^A JUANA BLANCO, sister of the before D^a Josefa, widow, age 23, living with them
MARGARITA SEGUI, daughter of Mig^l and of Clara Rosollo, age 22, wife of Vizente Laderolt, living with them

1793: St. Augustine and North River

17.

D[ᴺ] VALENTIN FITZPATRIK, son of D[ⁿ] Eugenio and of Dª Ana Gillard, age 33
Dᴬ ANA BOVIER, his wife, daughter of Dⁿ Ricardo and of Dª Maria, age 30
PEDRO FRAN^co, their son, age 6
JUAN HOPKINS GUDDEN, son of Fran^co and Maria Hopkins, age 9, not baptized, living with them
FRAN^co, his brother, age 7, not baptized, living with them
PEDRO BROWN, slave, living with them, [*no age given*]

[s.1–147]

18.

D[ᴺ] MIG^L LORENZO JINANDY [?], son of D[ⁿ] Domingo and Dª Margarita de San Lorenzo, age 42
Dᴬ JUANA TORRES, his wife, daughter of Rafael and of Dª Catalina Bernal, age 43
  10 slaves, 4 baptized

19.

Dᴬ PHELIPA LLANEZ, daughter of Pedro and of Ana Resco, widow, age 42
THOMAS ESCALONA, son of Joaquin and of the said [Phelipa], single, age 23
Dᴬ JOSEFA, his sister, single, age 20
JOAQUIN, brother, age 9
  1 female slave, convert
Dᴺ JUAN JOSEF DEL TORO, son of Juan and of Rosalia Ponze de Leon, age 43
Dᴬ RAFAELA ESCALONA, his wife, daughter of Joaquin and Phelipa Llanez, age 22
FERNANDA ESCALONA, their daughter, age 2
THOMOSA MARGARITA, her sister, age 3 months
  1 female negro living with them, not baptized

20.

D[ᴺ] JOSEF DE ORTEGAS, auditor, son of Dⁿ Fran^co and of Dª Maria Dias, age 36
Dᴬ MARIA IGNACIA ASSUNCIN [*sic*], his wife, daughter of Dⁿ Agustin and of Maria Ignª Garcia, age 31
MARIA JOSEFA, their daughter, age 5
IGNACIA ANTᴬ, her sister, age 3
JUANA NEPOMUCINA, her sister, age 1
  7 slaves, all baptized

21.

Dᴬ ANA MACDONNEL, daughter of D[ⁿ] Almiro and of Marg^ta Gouson, maried, her husband absent, age 32
THOMAS HOUGHTON, son of Thomas and of the said Ana, age 7
PATRICIO GORJE, his brother, age 5

―――――――――――――― 1793: St. Augustine and North River

22.
D[N] JORJE FLEMING, son of D\` Thomas and D\` Maria Welsh, age 32
D\` SOFIA MARIA PHELIPINA FACIO, his wife, daughter of D\` Fran^co Facio and of D\` Ur\` Mag^na [no surname given], age 26

[s.2-147]

23.
D^N MAN^L VELEZ, son of D[n] Bern^do and of D\` Fran^ca Gomez, single, age 35

24.
Vacant house belonging to the king

25.
D[N] PEDRO DIAZ BERRIO, son of D[n] Salvador and of D\` Maria Ant\` de Palma, age 39, his wife absent
    1 male slave, baptized

26.
ANT° DE PALMA, son of Juan and of Elvira Quintero, age 32
MARGARITA MACFEAL, his wife, daughter of Paulo and of Margarita Win, age 24
JUANA ELVIRA, their daughter, age 8
JUAN, her brother, age 5
MARIA, sister, age 4
    one female slave, not baptized

27.
ANT° [BERTA], son of Fran^co and of Mariana Arbisola, age 33
MARIA SANZ, his wife, daughter of Esteban and of Micaela Hern^z, age 26
CATALINA MIR, daughter of Maria by a previous husband, age 9
MICAELA MIR, her sister, age 6
MARIANA BERTA, daughter of Antonio and of Maria, age 3
    3 slaves, converts
LORENZO BERTA, brother of Ant°, single, age 37 [31?], living with them
JOSEF BATALINI, son of Juan Bautista and of Dominga Arnez, single, age 51, living with them

28.
D[N] MATEO GUADARAMA, son of Don Juan de Acosta and of D\` Fran^ca Padron, age 50
D\` BRIGIDA GOMEZ, his wife, daughter of D[n] Josef and Inez Mend^z, age 19
THOMAS, male slave [no age given]

[continued on next page]

1793: St. Augustine and North River

28. (cont'd)
JUAN BAUT^A, male slave, baptized [*no age given*]
MARIA DE LOS DOLORES, not baptized, slave [*no age given*]

[s.1–148]

JUAN ANT° GUADARAMA, nephew of Mateo, single, age 23
JOSEF DULZET, son of Pedro and of Maria Sceret, single, age 32, living with them

29.
D[N] RAFAEL DIAS, son of Josef and of Micaela Fuentes, age 46
MARIA DE LOS DOLORES MIRANDA, his wife, daughter of Diego and Margarita Rivero, age 27
MARIA ANICETA VALDEZ, orphan, age 10, living with them

30.
D[N] DOMINGO MARTINELY, son of Juan and of Petrona Povriti, age 34
D^A MARIANA CAVEDO, his wife, daughter of Santiago and of Inez Victurina, age 28
JUAN, their son, age 12
SANTIAGO, his brother, age 9
PETRONA, sister, age 7
JAIME, male mulatto, age 4
MARGARITA, slave, convert [*no age given*]

31.
LUIS BUCHANTINI, son of Mig^l and of Rosa Piumbi, age 43
CATALINA COLL, his wife, daughter of Bartolomeo and of Josefa Cintas, age 29
ANT^A MANUSI, daughter of Jose and of Juana Rio, age 11, living with them

32.
BARTOLOMEO LOPEZ, son of Andres and of Juana Triay, widower, age 38
CHRISTOBAL, their son, age 11
ANDRES, his brother, age 10
JUANA, sister, age 7

33.
JUAN BARBER, son of Fran^co and of Francisca Garcia, age 29
MARIA ROSA SEGUI, wife, daughter of Diego and Juana Castel, age 15

───────────────────────── 1793: St. Augustine and North River

Part 2: St. Charles Street

34.

ANT⁰ MAESTRE, son of Bartolomeo and of Antª Roquer, age 41
[s.2-148]
CATALINA NICKLERON, his wife, daughter of Guillermo and of Juana Daly, age 30
BARTOLOMEO MARCELINI, their son, age 1 month
    1 female slave, convert
ANTª ROQUER, daughter of Ant⁰ and of Antª Alez, mother of the said Ant⁰ Maestre, widow, age 66
ROSA MORRISON, daughter of Mig¹ and Mˢ Morrison, orphan, age 12, living with them

35.

Vacant house

36.

ANT⁰ CUELLO, son of Diego and of Antonia Perez, widower, age 67
ANT⁰ CUELLO, his son, age 17, single
MARIA MANUELA, his daughter, married, her husband absent, age 16
MARIA AGUSTINA, free negress, single, age 39

37.

FRANᶜᵒ BLASI, son of Franᶜᵒ and of Maria Barcelo, age 34, married, his wife absent
JUAN BLASI, his son, age 6

38.

ANT⁰ SAMBIAS, son of Juan and of Margarita Cardona, age 31
ANA HINDSMAN, his wife, daughter of Ant⁰ and of Barbara Hrasburgz, age 28
JUAN, their son, age 3
ANT⁰, his brother, age 1
ISABEL MOTT, daughter of Jonas and of Maria Hindsman, single, age 16

39.

PEDRO FONTANEL, son of Josef and of Antª Lago, age 32
MARIA LUISA RODRIGᶻ, daughter of Simon and of Alecia Wedington, age 33

1793: St. Augustine and North River

40.
GORJE LONG, son of Mateo and of Catalina Mongumrey, age 40, Protestant
CHRISTINA MATHEWSON, his wife, daughter of Juan and of Ana McCrey, age 35, Protestant
WINIFRED MCINTOSH, daughter of another husband and Christiana, age 16
[s.1-149]
MATEO, her brother, age 2, all Protestants

41.
LORENZO LLANEZ, son of Juan and of Barbara Villegas, widower, age 42
BARBARA, daughter of Lorenzo and of his deceased wife, age 3
JOSEF RAFAEL, son of Lorenzo and of Juana Alb^z, age 13
    1 female slave, not baptized

42.
D[N] PEDRO GARCIA, son of Clemente and of Dominga Garcia, age 35
D^A JOSEFA FEMENIAS, his wife, daughter of Jaime and of Josefa Coll, age 18
    1 female slave, convert

43.
FRAN^{co} ESTACHOLI, son of Domingo and of Barb^a Leon, age 46
MARIA PETROS, his wife, daughter of Bartolomeo and of Ant^a Lubera, age 36
DOMINGO, their son, age 18, single
BARTOLOMEO, his brother, age 16, single
BARBARA, sister, age 11

44.
D^A MARGARITA GEYNON, daughter of Andres and Maria Geynon, widow, age 47
MARIA ANA TREAN, daughter of Margarita and her deceased huband, age 8
GILLERMO[sic], her brother, 6
    6 slaves, none baptized
ANT^o PELLICIER, son of Fran^{co} and Margari^{ta} Femenias, single, age 18, apprentice

45.
D^N MANUEL SOLANA, son of Phelipe and of Geronima Cerano, age 49
D^A MARIA MAESTRE, his wife, daughter of Bartolomeo and of An^a Roquer, age 27
PHELIP SOLANO, their son, age 11
MANUEL, his brother, age 3
BARTOLOMEO, his brother, age 1
LORENZO, son, age 7-18 [?]
    10 slaves, 5 baptized
D^N BERNARDO O'CALLAGHAN, son of [blank], single, no age given

1793: St. Augustine and North River

[s.2-149]

46.
JOSEF FONTANEL, son of Josef and of Ant^a Lago, age 38
MARIA ASTON, his wife, daughter of Edwardo and of Dorotea Higginbothora, age 18
FRAN^{CA} DE PAULA, their daughter, age 1
ESTEBAN CASADA, son of Juan and of [not given], single, age 23, living with them

47.
D^N RAMON DE FUENTES, son of Don Ant° and of D^a Gregoria Silva, age 38
D^A MARIA PENY [PERY?], his wife, daughter of Marmduke and of Maria Hazard, age 19
ANT°, their son, age 5

48.
D^[N] GONZALEO ZAMORANO, son of Dⁿ Fran^{co} and Joaquina Gonzales, age 52
D^A FRAN^{CA} DEL CORRAL, his wife, daughter of Don Felix and of D^a Juana de Dios Menocal, age 26
FRAN^{CA}, daughter, age 8
PETRONA, her sister, age 7
MARIA DE LA O., sister, age 5
JOSEF JUAN DE SAGA–UN[?], age 2
2 slaves, 1 baptized
FRAN^{CA} DE SALES HONYCUTT, daughter of Agustin and of Mª Smith, single, age 20, living with them

49.
D^N MARIANO DE LASAGA, son of Dⁿ Joaquin and D^a Maria Rosa Dias, age 34
D^A INEZ GENERINO, his wife, daughter of D^[n] Ant° and Inez Cabedo, age 16
3 slaves, not baptized

50.
D^N PEDRO COUFACIO, son of Theodoro and of Marta Notachisa, age 41
D^A INEZ CABEDO, his wife, daughter of Santiago and Inez Victorina, age 43
MARTA, their daughter, age 14
PRAREDIS, their daughter, age 12
JACOB, their son, age 6
D^A MARIA ROSA GENERINO, daughter of Dⁿ Ant°, the first husband of above D^a Inez, single, age 18

[s.1-150]

9 slaves, 5 baptized

1793: St. Augustine and North River

51.
MARIANA INDORI, daughter of Rafael and of Antª Casanovas, widow, age 34
MARCOS ANDREU, son of above and of her deceased husband, age 11
ANTª, their daughter, age 9
RAFAEL, her brother, age 7
ANTª PURCEL, daughter of Mariana and her first husband, age 13
    1 female slave, not baptized
PEDRO FURNELLES, son of Juan and Juana Quintana, age 33, living with them
FRAN^{co} PONZ, son of Josef and of Maria Capella, age 38, living with them

52.
ANT° CANTER, son of Agustin and of Prarides Venent, age 39, absent
CATALINA COSTA, his wife, daughter of Domingo and of Maria Ambros, age 30
AGUSTIN, their son, age 17, absent
DOMINGO, his brother, age 13
MARIA, sister, age 8
PATRICIO, brother, age 7
    4 slaves, 2 baptized

53.
JOSEF PESO DE BURGO, son of Pedro and of Geronima Camugina, age 34
MARIA MABRITI, his wife, daughter of Nicolas and of Maria Costa, age 18
PEDRO JOSEF ANTONIO, their son, age 2 months
    15 slaves, 4 baptized

54.
JOSEF PONZ, son of Josef and of Maria Triay, age 62
MARIA TRIAY, his wife, daughter of Juan and of Antª Campos, age 56
DIMAS, their son, age 10
CATALINA, a female slave, age 19

[s.2-150]

55.
MARIA BEATRIZ SANCHEZ, daughter of Dⁿ Fran^{co} Xavier Sanchez and of the free mulatto Maria Beatriz Stone, single, age 18
ANA, her sister, age 16, single
CATALINA ROSA, her sister, age 14, single
JOSEF, brother, age 21 [sic], single
ANT°, brother, age 11
MARIA DE LA CONCEPCION, sister, age 9
MARIA DEL CARMEN, sister, age 9 [sic]
FRAN^{co} MATEO, brother, age 7
    5 slaves, 1 baptized

1793: St. Augustine and North River

56.
MARTIN HERNANDEZ, son of Gaspar and of Margarita Triay, age 38
DOROTEA GOMILA, his wife, daughter of Josef and of Catalina Gomila, age 31
MARGARITA, their daughter, age 10
CATALINA, her sister, age 7
JOSEF, her brother, age 5
GASPAR, brother, age 3
    7 slaves, 3 baptized
JOSEF GOMILA, son of Joaquin and of Catalina Flusa, widower, age 66

57.
FRAN^{co} XAVIER MIRANDA, son of Diego and of Juana Margarita Ribero, age 28
MARIA ANDREA SANCHEZ, his wife, daughter of Josef and of Ant^a Espinosa, age 23
MARIA JULIANA RAMONA, their daughter, age 4
MARIA MANUELA, her sister, age 4 days
    1 male slave, not baptized

58.
D$^{[n]}$ LORENZO RODRIG^z, son of Pedro and of Ana Maria Escobal, age 61
D^A ISABEL CASILDA PUIMA, his wife, daughter of Maria, age 52
ANDREA, a male slave
TOMAS, a male slave
ANT^o, slave, baptized

[s.1–151]

59.
PEDRO LA FEBRE, son of Phelipe Man^l and of Margarita Bohan, age 38
MARIA GUTREAU, his wife, daughter of Martin and of Ana Belisle, age 18
PEDRO MAN^L, their son, age 2 months
ANA BELISLE, daughter of Alexandro and of Maria Blan^{ca}, mother of the said Maria, widow, age 58, living with them
PEDRO CASALY, son of Vicente and of Catalina Redivetes, apprentice, age 19

60.
D$^{[n]}$ JUAN LESLIE, son of D$^{[n]}$ Alexandro and D^a Ana Duff, age 40, Protestant
D^A ISABEL KEAN, his wife, daughter of D$^{[n]}$ Juan and of D^a Rebecca Pengree, age 21, Protestant
ISABEL ROSA, their daughter, age 8 months, baptized
D^N JOSEF CLARKE, son of D$^{[n]}$ Thomas and D^a Honoria Cummings, age 18, apprentice
D$^{[n]}$ JUAN ELLERBEE, son of Thomas and of Sarah Mulcartre, age 26, single, Protestant
    14 slaves, 5 baptized.

1793: St. Augustine and North River

61.
JUAN BAUTISTA WITEN, free negro [*no age given*]
MARIA RAFAELA, free negress, his wife [*no age given*]
FRAN^{co}, their son, age 13
MARIA RAFAELA, his sister, age 11
MARGARITA, free negress, age 12, living with them

62.
D$^{[n]}$ MAN^L FERNAND^z BENDICHO, son of D^n Fran^{co} and D^a Fran^{ca} Bendicho, age 34
D^A MARIA RAFAELA RODRIG^z, his wife, daughter of D^n Lorenzo and of Isabel Puima, age 23
     5 slaves, 3 baptized

63.
D$^{[n]}$ MANUEL ROMERO, son of Juan Fran^{co} and of [*not given*]
D^A ISABEL CASIMIRA RODRIG^z, his wife, daughter of D$^{[n]}$ Lorenzo and of D^a Isabel Puima, age 25
PAULA PLUTARCA, their daughter, age 6
MAN^L MAURICIO, brother, age 4

[*s. 2–151*]

64.
D^N DOMINGO REYES, son of D$^{[n]}$ Gabril and D^a Maria Luisa Riso, widower, age 39
DOMINGO, son of [Domingo] and of D^a Man^a Belen Chacon, deceased, age 9
JOSEF, his brother, age 6
FRAN^{co}, his brother, age 3

65.
GASPAR MARTEL, son of Blas and of Juana Angela Riso, age 37
ANGELA ROSI, his wife, daughter of Josef and of Fran^{ca} Sanz, age 17
JUANA, their daughter, age 2

66.
JUAN PURCEL, son of Jaime and Isabel Druly, single, age 38
JORJE POWEL, son of Juan and of Sarah Clapton, single, age 30, Protestant

67.
MARGARITA, free negress, not baptized [*no age given*]
JUANA, free negress [*no age given*]

68.
LUCIA, free negress, baptized [*no age given*], with six free negroes, not baptized [*no ages given*]

―――――――――― 1793: St. Augustine and North River

69.
D^N JOSEF MARIA GOMEZ, son of Pedro and of Maria Rodrig^z, age 48
D^A INEZ FRAN^{CA} MENDEZ, his wife, daughter of Pedro and of Catalina Ruiz, age 39
JOSEF, their son, age 16
JUAN, his brother, age 15
NICOLAS, brother, age 14
EUSEBIO, brother, age 11
MARIA, sister, age 6
BERNARDO, brother, age 4
    1 female slave, baptized
ELENA ARTIAGA, daughter of Benito and of Geromina Escalona, single, age 43
LUCIA MENDEZ, daughter of Pedro and of Catalina Ruez del Camo [sic], age 36
FELIX JOSEF MONTE, son of Alexander and of Maria Mendez, age 5
JOSEF ANT°, brother [no age given]
    1 female slave, baptized
                                                   [s.1-152]

70.
JUAN HERNAND^z, son of Gaspar and of Margarita Triay, age 40
MARGARITA PONZ, his wife, daughter of Juan and Margarita Ridavetes, age 17
MARGARITA, their daughter, age 1
MAGDALENA PONZ, daughter of Juan and of Maria Juso, age 32, married, her husband absent
JUAN MACHOQUI, son of Joaquin and of the said Ponz, age 19, single

71.
D^A HONORIA CLARKE, daughter of Sant° [Cummings] and D^a Margarita Madan, widow, age 47
D^A MARGARITA, daughter of D$^{[n]}$ Thomas and of said Honoria, single, age 21
D$^{[N]}$ CARLOS GUALTERO, her brother, age 20
    12 slaves, 6 baptized

72.
ANT° MONTES DE OCA, son of Bartolome and of Josefa Rodrig^z, age 52
PAULA TORRES, his wife, daughter of Bernardo and of Juana Campan, age 44
JOSEFA MONTES DE OCA, their daughter, age 4
MATEO LORENZO, son of [Paula] and her previous husband Mateo, age 21, single
JUANA LORENZO, sister, age 18

73.
LUISA GONZALES, daughter of Roque and of Juana Suarez, widow, age 41
JUAN ACOSTA, son of [not given] in Cartagena
BASILIA DELGADO, daughter of Juan and of Petrona Gomez, age 23, wife of the cited Acosta

81

1793: St. Augustine and North River

74.
JUAN PAREDES, son of Ramon and of Margarita Ensenada, age 37
ISABEL RIDAVETS, his wife, daughter of Juan and of Fran^ca Olivas, age 34
JUANA, their daughter, age 8
MARGARITA PAREDES, daughter of Josef and of Ant^a Hull [Hill?], age 6, living with them
PEDRO VADEL, son of I^se and Jos^a Ponz, age 13

[s.2-152]

75.
PEDRO RODRIG^z, son of Lorenzo and of Catalina Ruiz, single, age 36
1 male slave, not baptized

76.
DIEGO HERNAND^z, son of Diego and of Victoria Vives, age 33
MARIANA REYES, his wife, daughter of Juan and of Juana Maria Alberti, age 15

77.
DIEGO SEGUI, son of Juan and of Maria Ferrer, age 46
JUANA CASTEL, his wife, daughter of Bartolome and of Agueda Segui, age 36
JUANA, their daughter, age 8
DIEGO, her brother, age 6
CATALINA, sister, age 4
AGUEDA, sister, age 2

78.
JUAN CARERAS, son of Juan and of Margarita Perpal, age 46
MARIA TRIAY, his wife, daughter of Josef and of Maria Truol, age 26
MARGARITA, their daughter, age 8
MARIA, her sister, age 6
JUAN, brother, age 2

79.
D[N] JACOBO HAMILTON HALL, son of "Juan and of Tecla Ana (daughter of the said Juan)" [sic], age 26 years, Protestant
D^A SARAH SMITH, his wife, daughter of Jacobo and Ana Piles, age 21, Protestant
TECLA ANA, their daughter, age 1 month

80.
DOMINGO HEDSORCOPLI, son of Teodoro and Catalina Catrinaricha, widower, age 38
JUANA HERNAND^z, daughter of Pedro and of Juana Ristoa, married, her husband absent, age 28
ANT^A PEREGRIN, daughter of Bartolome and of the above [Juana], age 7
JUANA, her sister, age 5

1793: St. Augustine and North River

[s.1-153]

Part Three: Hospital Street

81.
D[ⁿ] THOMAS TRAVERS, son of Juan and of Dª Ana Carrel, age 35
Dᴬ MARIA FITZGERALD, his wife, daughter of D[ⁿ] Geraldo and Dª Isabel Coonon, age 29
ANA, their daughter, age 11
JUAN, their son, age 9
MARIA, sister, age 2 months
        8 slaves, 1 baptized

82.
JORJE BECKHONSRE, Indian, age 36, Protestant
MARIA HARRIS, age 63, mulatto, Protestant

83.
Dᴺ JUAN FANTO[?] DE SALAS, son of Juan and of Maria Ceveris, age 63, widower
CLEMENTE, son of Juan and of Juana Sanchez de la Rosa, widower, age 35
JUAN ANTº, son of the [above] and of Juana Margᵗᵃ, deceased, age 3 months

84.
D[ⁿ] MIGᴸ O'REILLY, Priest
D[ⁿ] JUAN O'REILLY, his brother, age 22, single
D[ⁿ] LORENZO O'REILLY, nephew, age 23, single
        1 female slave

85.
JOAQUIN SANCHEZ, son of Diego and of Franᶜᵃ Acosta, age 32
MARIA RITA BRAVO, his wife, daughter of Thomas and Maria de los A[n]gelos Prado, age 22
JUAN JOSEF, their son, age 5
JOSEF, his brother, age 1
ANA CARILA, daughter of Franᶜᵒ and of Franᶜᵃ Rodrigᶻ, widow, age 48
JOSEF MARIA, son of the above Ana and of her deceased husband, age 19

86.
JUAN GUTIERROS, son of Andres and of Franᶜᵃ Fernandᶻ, age 29
Dᴬ MARIA ESTEFANOPOLY, his wife, daughter of Nicolas and Juana Marin, age 18
ANDRES, their son, age 4 months

1793: St. Augustine and North River

[s.2-153]

87.

ANDRES XIMENES, son of Mig^l and of Rosa Clavero, age 40
JUANA PALLICER, his wife, daughter of Fran^{co} and Juana Villa, age 16
JOSEF, their son, age 3 months
    1 male slave not baptized

88.

JOSEF KEVY, age 43
BARBARA BOBINSON [ROBINSON], his wife, daughter of Mig^l and of Margarita Davison, age 30
JUAN, their son, age 8

89.

JUAN PARKINSON, son of Edwardo and Maria O'Brien, single, age 26, Protestant
JUAN DEWECES[?], mulatto apprentice, age 16, not baptized

90.

D[N] BERNARDO SEGUI, son of Bernardo and of Juana Alcina, age 49
D^A AGUEDA VILLALONGA, his wife, daughter of Bartolome and Agueda Mely, age 39
ANT^A, their daughter, age 16, single
CLARA, sister, age 14, single
BARTOLOME, brother, age 12
BLANCA, sister, age 10
BERNARDO, brother, age 8
MARIA, sister, age 6
LORENZO, brother, age 4
    7 slaves, 2 baptized

91.

D^N FRAN^{co} RUIS DEL CANTO, son of Juan and of Geronima Escalona, age 63
D^A FRAN^{CA} DE ITA Y SALAZAR, his wife, daughter of Geronimo and of Juana Havero, age 53
FRAN^{co}, their son, age 17, single
LUISA, sister, age 13
JUAN, brother, age 10
    4 slaves, all confirmed
DIEGO CESCALOMA, son of Man^l and of Ant^a Quinomez, single, age 61

---------- 1793: St. Augustine and North River

[s.1-154]

Part 4: St. George Street

92.

ANT° CANOBAS, son of Ant° and of Juana Redevetes, age 37
CATALINA, his wife, daughter of Bartolome Maestre and Ant^a Ruger, age 34
BARTOLOMEO, their son, age 5
MARTIN, his brother, age 1

93.

VICENTE CASALY, son of Ant° and of Agueda Casaly, age 46, widow
1 female slave, not baptized

94.

BARTOLOME SUAREZ, son of Juan and of Juana Martinez, age 22
AGUEDA CASALY, his wife, daughter of Vicente and Catalina Redavetes, age 21

95.

JOSEF BELTIDO, son of Fran^{co} and of Josefa Moreno, age 40
ANT^A FORNALIS, daughter of Juan and of Clara Ponz, age 41
JUAN [*no surname*], son of Ant^a and of her deceased husband, age 12
CATALINA, his sister, age 11
CLARA, sister, age 6

96.

GASPAR PAPI, son of Mig^l and of Catalina Auas, age 42
ANA PONZ, his wife, daughter of Mig^l and of Fran^{ca} Coll, age 28
CATALINA, their daughter, age 5
MARIA, her sister, age 4
ANA, sister, age 1
2 slaves, not baptized

97.

NICOLAS ESTEPLANOPLI, son of Elias and of Marta, age 45
JUANA MARIN, his wife, daughter of Fran^{co} Marin and of Magdalina Escudero, age 39
JUANA, their daughter, age 10
FRAN^{co}, her brother, age 6

1793: St. Augustine and North River

[s.2-154]

98.

D[n] ALEXANDRO LESLIE, son of Alexandro and Lucia Danbrooks, age 28, Protestant
D[a] JUANA WELSH, his wife, daughter of Guillermo and of D[a] Ana Bowin [?], age 25, Protestant
JUANA HARRIOT, their daughter, age 5, baptized
ALEXANDRO, her brother, age 3, baptized
D[a] ISABEL BRACIEN, daughter of Guillermo and of Catalina Norwart, widow, age 20, Protestant
ELIZA LESLIE, daughter of [Isabel] and D[n] Alexandro, her deceased husband, age 5, Protestant
CARLOTA, her sister, age 3, baptized
D[a] LUCIA LESLIE, daughter of D[n] Alexandro and D[a] Lucia Danbrooks, age 16
    1 male slave, not baptized

99.

D[n] NICOLAS RODRIGUEZ, son of D[n] Loren[zo] and of D[a] Isabel Casilda y Puima, age 38
D[a] MARIA RAFAELA SCOTT, his wife, daughter of D[n] Juan and Sarah Briton, age 24

100.

D[n] JOSEF DE ZUBRANETA, son of Don Domingo and of D[a] Maria de Casas, age 28
D[a] MARIA GERMANA DE SORIA, his wife, daughter of D[n] Vicente de Soria and of D[a] Josefa Fernand[z], age 18
LORENZO JULIANO MAN[l], their son, age 1
    1 female slave, convert

101.

JUAN RODRIG[z], son of Man[l] and of Josefa Ruiz, age 39
FRAN[ca] AGUILAN, his wife, daughter of Juan and of Melchora Ramos, age 21
THOMAS, their son, age 7
DIONISIA, his sister, age 5
DOMINGO RAFAEL, her brother, age 2
MERCHORA [sic] RAMOS, daughter of Thomas and Agueda Vera, age 46, widow
TOMAS AQUILLIAM, son of said [Melchora], single, age 17

[s.1-155]

102.

JUAN FRAN[co] ARNAU, son of Juan and of Isabel Becardo, age 35 [39?]
ISABEL MULA, his wife, daughter of Bernardo and of Catalina Villa, age 39
ISABEL, their daughter, age 8
JUAN, her brother, age 7

───────────── 1793: St. Augustine and North River

103.
D[N] BARTOLOME DE GASINO Y LERNEN, son of D^n Santiago and of D^a Ana Perren [Lerren?], age 33, single

104.
D[N] FRAN^{co} ENTARGO, son of Man^l and of Isabel Rodrig^z, age 34
D^A CATALINA NIFUELAS, his wife, daughter of Josef and Catalina Cantal, age 35
JUAN BLAS, their son, age 14
JUAN ANT°, brother, age 12
CLARA, their daughter, age 10
FRAN^{co}, brother, age 7
MARIA, sister, age 6
                1 male slave, convert

105.
D^A JUANA MARGARITA RIVERO, daughter of Fran^{co} and of Isabel Rod^z, widow, age 50
ANT^A, daughter of [Juana] and of her deceased husband, age 30
PEDRO MIRANDA, brother, age 18, single
SILVESTRE, brother, age 16, single
MARIA DE LA CONCEP^{ON}, sister, age 15, single
PEDRO JOSEF, brother, age 11
DIEGO, brother, age 6
ANT° ALMANSA, son of Mariano and of Maria Miranda, age 4

106.
D[N] SEBASTIAN VENAZALUCE, son of D^n Juan and of Maria Esperania, age 33
MARIA DEL CARMEN RODRIG^z, his wife, daughter of D^n Lorenzo and D^a Isabel Puima, age 30
MANUELA, their daughter, age 4
MANUEL, brother, 1
ISABELLA, sister, age 3 months

                                                [s.2–155]
107.

LORENZO CAPO, son of Ant° and of Rafaela Fabregas, age 48
D^A MARGARITA CANE, his wife, daughter of Bartolome and of Agueda Seguera, age 20
MARIA DE LOS DOLORES, their daughter, age 2
RAFAELA, daughter of Lorenzo and of another wife, age 12
ANT°, her brother, age 10
                1 male mulatto living with them, baptized

1793: St. Augustine and North River

108.

EL S^{OR} D^[N] JUAN NEPOMUCENO DE QUESADA, Gov^{or}, [*no age given*]
LA S^{RA} MARIA JOSEFA ARANGO, his wife [*no age given*]
D^[N] VICENTE, their son, age 11
D^[N] RAFAEL, his brother, age 8
D^[A] MANUELA, his sister, age 3
D^[A] MARIA DE LA ASENCION, age 2 months
D^[N] VICENTE MEXIAS, steward, single, age 31
    9 slaves, all baptized

109.

D^N JUAN M^CQUIEN, absent, son of Dⁿ Juan and of D^a Ana Dalton, age 42, married, his wife absent
    3 slaves, not baptized

110.

BARTOLOME LLUFRIO, son of Constantino and of Ursula Alberti, age 41
ANT^A MAESTRE, his wife, daughter of Bartolome and of Ant^a Roger, age 38
URSULA, their daughter, age 8
CONSTANTINO, brother, age 6
JUAN ANT^O, brother, age 3

111.

D^[N] PHELIPE AGUIRRE, son of Dⁿ Fran^{co} and of D^a Maria Josefa Sasgarse, single, age 28

112.

D^N JUAN BAUT^A FERREYNA, son of Ant^o and of Gracia Maria Fonteoa, age 29
D^A ISABEL NIXON, his wife, daughter of Juan and Ana Ursula Andrade, age 28
JUAN, son, age 10
MARIA, his sister, age 7
FRAN^{CO} LORENZO, her brother, age 2
    1 female slave, baptized

[s.1–155a]

D^A ANA URSULA ANDRADE, daughter of Henrique and of Josefa Camena, widow, age 45
ANA NIXON, daughter of Juan and of above widow Andrade, single, age 22
INHARIA, daughter of Ana [Andrade], age 3

_____ 1793 : St. Augustine and North River

113.

D[N] GERARDO FORRASTER, son of Don Patricio and of D^a Brig^{da} MacDonnel, age 56
D^A DONISIA HULL, his wife, daughter of D^n Ant^o and of D^a Susanah Kean, age 34
SUSANAH, their daughter, age 12
THOMAS, brother, age 13
ISABEL, sister, age 10
GERARDO, brother, age 6
D^A SUSANAH KEAN, mother of Donisia, widow [*no age given*]
D^A SUSANAH KEAN HUNTER, daughter of Alexandro and of D^a Sarah Hull, single, age 17, living with them
    4 slaves, not baptized

114.

ANA BARNETT, daughter of Thomas and Isabel Jomon, widow, age 28, Protestant
FRAN^{CA}, daughter of Ana and of her deceased husband Fran^{co} Roche [*no age given*]
CLARA, sister, age 6, baptized
JOSEF, brother, age 4, baptized
ANA, sister, age 1, baptized

115.

DIEGEO CARRERAS, son of Juan and of Maria Triay, age 30
CLARA PASCETI, his wife, daughter of Andres and of Getrudiz Ponz, age 20
MARIA, daughter, age 5
GETRUDIS, sister, age 2
    1 female slave, convert
ANDRES PASCETI, son of Thomas and of [*no first name*] Sangarote, age 47
MARIA CASTELL, his wife, daughter of Bartolome and of Agueda Segui, age 33
ANDRES, their son, age 7

[s.2-155a]

BARTOLOMEO, brother, age 2
THOMAS, son of Andres and of his first wife Getrud^z Ponz, single, age 17
MAGDALENA, sister, age 15
GETRUD^z, sister, age 12
AGUEDA SEGUI, daughter of the said [Maria Castell] and her former husband Juan Segui, age 10
    4 slaves, 1 baptized

89

1793: St. Augustine and North River

116.
JUAN CAVIO, son of Santiago and of Inez Vestorin, age 31
JUANA SEGUI, his wife, daughter of D[n] Bernardo and Agueda Villalonga, age 22
INEZ, their daughter, age 6
INEZ VICTORINA, mother of Juan, widow, age 62

117.
JUAN VILLALONGA, son of Bartolome and of Agueda Melia, age 47
MARIAN CARDONA, his wife, daughter of Lorenzo and of Margarita Mila, age 41
AGUEDA VILLALONGA, daughter, age 12
MARIA, sister, age 7
BARTOLOMEO, brother, age 4
  2 slaves, 1 baptized

118.
D[N] THOMAS HASSETT, priest
[illegible], vicar and clergyman
  2 slaves, married

119.
JOSEF COSTA, son of Domingo and of Maria Bross, age 26
MARGARITA VILLALONGA, his wife, daughter of Juan and of Mariana Cardona, age 17
  1 male slave, not baptized

120.
D[M] GILLERMO M{c}ENNIS, son of Juan and of Isabel Searle, age 57, widower
D^A ISABEL M^AC ERONES [M{c}ENNIS?], daughter [no age given]
D^A MARIA HACKET, married to D^n Guillermo Gernon, absent, age 28
THOMAS GERNON, son, age 4

[s.1–156]

JUAN, his brother, age 2
GUILLERMO MURRO, son of said Maria and of previous husband Jorje, age 11
HANA, his sister, age 8
  1 female slave, convert

121.
SEBASTIAN HORTEGA, son of Sebastian and of Ana Xeres, age 42
ANA MARIA CAVEDO, his wife, daughter of Sant° and of Inez Victoria, age 42

[household continued on next page]

1793 : St. Augustine and North River

121. (cont'd)
SEBASTIAN, their son, age 18, single
SANTIAGO, brother, age 15, single
BERNARDO, brother, age 7
INEZ, sister, age 4
MARIANO, brother, age 2
    1 female slave, not baptized

122.
MATIAS PONZ, son of Fran^{co} and of Agueda Euget, age 39
JUANA VILLA, his wife, daughter of Pedro and of Ant^a Fiol, age 36
ANT^A, their daughter, age 12
AGUEDA, her sister, age 9
FRAN^{co}, brother, age 7
PEDRO, brother, age 5

123.
JOSEF CORTES, a child [sic] of the M^l Hosp^l [Military Hospital] de Galia, age 46

124.
JAIME PRATTS, son of Fran^{co} and of Maria Campos
MARGARITA VIVOS, his wife, daughter of Magino and of Juana Vinz, age 44

125.
DOMETRIO TUDELACHE, native of Canora, age 45
MARIA PARLA, his wife, daughter of Juan and of Catalina Brass, age 57
NICOLAS, their son, single, age 22
MIGUEL COSTA, son of [above] Maria Parla and Domingo, prior husband, age 30
MARIA DREMARICHE, his wife, daughter of Domingo and Catalina Femenias, age 18
DOMINGO, their son, age 3
    1 male slave, not baptized
                              [s.2–156]

126.
D^[N] JUAN SANCHEZ, son of Juan and of Catalina de Soto, age 45
MARIA CASTANEDA, his wife, daughter of Gaspar and Sebastina de Bargas, age 51
MARIA SANCHEZ, their daughter, age 14
MARIA DEL ROSARIO, her sister, age 8
    4 slaves, baptized

127.
D^A EUGENIA DE ITA Y SALACAR, daughter of Geronimo and Juana Avero, widow,
    age 56
    1 male slave, baptized

1793: St. Augustine and North River

128.
D[n] TUDEO DE ARIBAS, son of D[n] Raymundo and D[a] Ursela de Avero, age 26
D[A] MARIA GRACIA PERPAL, his wife, age 21
URSELA, their daughter, age 2
MARIA ISABEL, her sister, age 2 months
    2 slaves, 1 baptized

129.
D[N] PEDRO JOSEF SALZEDO, Com[te] de Artell[a], [no age given]
D[A] MARIA DOLOR[s] GALEN, his wife, daughter of D[n] Juan and of Da Manuela Inero [no age given]
MARIA JOSEFA WELON, daughter of Juan and Juana Allon, single, age 16
CATALINA XIMINEZ, daughter of Rafaela and of Maria Ramillera, age 8
    2 slaves, baptized

130.
MARIA TRIAY, daughter of Fran[co] and of Maria Englada, widow, age 56
    6 slaves, 4 baptized
FRAN[co] TRIAY, son of Juan and of [the above], age 41
MARIA SLOP, his wife, daughter of Pedro and of Juana Barcelo, age 19
MARIA, their daughter, age 2
JUAN, brother, age 2 months

[s.1–157]

131.
JUAN TRIAY, son of Juan and of Juana Ponz, age 39
JUANA XIMINEZ, his wife, daughter of Juan and of Barbara Ponz, age 39
JUAN, their son, age 12
FRAN[co], brother of the above, age 10
BARBARA, sister, age 4
JOSEF BAYA, son of Ant[o] and of the [above] Juana, age 15
    1 female slave, not baptized

132.
D[N] SEBASTIAN GARCIA, son of Juan and of Maria Sanchez, age 31
D[A] JOSEFA ORTEGAS, his wife, daughter of D[n] Josef and of D[a] Maria Castaneda, age 26

133.
DIEGO CLARKE, age 36 [sic], Protestant
MARGARITA, his wife, age 55 [sic], Protestant
    1 slave, not baptized

_____1793 : St. Augustine and North River

134.
Dᴬ LUISA ESCALONA, daughter of Alonzo and of Sebastiana Bargas, widow, age 65
MARIA DEL ROSARIO, slave [no age given]
FRANCISCA, daughter of above slave [no age given]
ANTº, slave [no age given]

135.
Dᴬ VICENTE MORENO, son of Dⁿ Antº and of Catalina Suarez, age 30
Dᴬ MELCHORA MINTERO, his wife, daughter of Dⁿ Pedro and of Dᵃ Maria de Cordoba, age 34
FERNANDO MARIA, their son, age 6
MARIA MANUELA, his sister, age 5
RAMON, brother, age 3
JUAN DE LA CRUX, brother, age 1
NICOLAS AGUSTIN, age 3

136.
RAFAELA XIMENEZ, son of Rafael and of Catalina Espineta, age 58
MARIA RAMILLERA, his wife, daughter of Domingo and of Esperansa Campos, age 41
MARIA, their daughter, age 13
RAFAEL, her brother, age 5 [sic]
ESPERANSA, age 10
GERONIMA, age 4

[s.2-157]

137.
D[ⁿ] JOSEF PONZ DE LEON, son of D[ⁿ] Franᶜᵒ and of Dᵃ Jacoba Puello, age 43
Dᴬ CATALINA DE PORRAS, his wife, daughter of Salbador and Juana Navarra, age 39
JOSEF, son, age 15
MANUELA, daughter, age 9
CIRIACO, her brother, age 7

138.
JOSEF CARRERAS, son of Pedro and of Margarita Campos, age 37
JUANA ANDREU, his wife, daughter of Juan and of Angela Caulas, age 45
MARIA, daughter, age 11
JUANA, her sister, age 7
ANGELA CAULAS, daughter of Antºand of Juana Ponz, widow, age 81
DOMINGO VALLS, son of Domingo and of the said Juana, single, age 22

139.
LUIS SOCHE, son of Juan and of Maria Ruiz, age [illegible]
ANTᴬ TREMOL, his wife, daughter of Pedro and Margarita Campos, age 31

93

1793: St. Augustine and North River

140.
JOSEF ESPINETA, son of Juan and of Juana Cintas, age 45
MARIA TRUAL, his wife, daughter of Sebastian and of Magdalena del Pozo, age 54
FRAN^{co}, son, age 26, single

141.
JUAN GONSOPLI, son of Gorje and of Maria Canela, age 42, widower
3 slaves, 1 baptized

142.
LUCIA PESO DE BURGO, daughter of Domingo and of Magdalena de Nuncio, widow, age 55
PEDRO PESO DE BURGO, son of Lucia and of her deceased husband Fran^{co}, age 18, single

143.
D^a NICOLASA GOMEZ, daughter of Pedro and of Maria Getrudiz Rodrig^z, widow, age 64
BARBARA, negro slave
BLOS, slave
RAFAEL, slave

[s.1–158]

144.
D^N FERNANDO DELANZA AREDONDO, son of Josef and D^a Teresa Aredondo, age 28
D^a ANT^a PERDOMO, wife, daughter of D^n Ignacio and Nicolasa Gomez, age 27
JOSEF, son, age 7
FERNANDO, brother, age 5
DOMINGA, his sister, age 2
DOROTEA, sister, age 4 months
D^N JOSEF FRIS [?], adjutant of the city

145.
FRAN^{co} ARNAU, son of Fran^{co} and of Ant^a Ponells, age 43
CLARA PRETOS, his wife, daughter of Santiago and of Fran^{ca} Pratt, age 42
FRAN^{co}, son, age 19, single
SANTIAGO, his brother, age 16, single
FRAN^{CA}, sister, age 12
CLARA, sister, age 5
DOMINGA, sister, age 3

_____ 1793 : St. Augustine and North River

Part 5: Dragoon Barracks Street

146.
PEDRO DE CALA, son of Lucas and of Juana, age 46
ANA MARIA DE LA DOLORES SEGUI, his wife, daughter of Juan and Isabel Segui, age 23
MAN¹ JOSEF, their son, age 4
ANTº, his brother, age 2
    2 slaves, 1 baptized

147.
JUAN PONZ, son of Antº and of Margarita Cardona, age 31
JUANA ANDREU, his wife, daughter of Antº and of Maria Olibera, age 21
MARIANA, daughter, age 2

148.
JUAN LORENZO, son of Juan and of Mariana Quintana, age 38
MARIA VILLA, his wife, daughter of Franᶜᵒ and of Maria Ferrer, age 34
[s.2–158]
MARIANA, their daughter, age 13
JUAN, her brother, age 11
ANTº, his brother, age 7
MAGDALENA, sister, age 3
MATHEO, brother, age 1 month

149.
ANTᴬ ESPINETA, daughter of [blank] and of Catalina Espineta, widow, age 28
MARGARITA, daughter of [above] and of her deceased husband, age 6

150.
ANTº JOSEF ALBERTI, son of Christobal and of Juana Maria Fabregas, age 48
JUAN, son of Josef and of his deceased wife Catalina Oliberas, age 13
FRANᶜᴬ, his sister, age 11
JUANA MARIA, sister, age 4

151.
ANTº MEINA, son of Mig¹ and of Catalina Alcina, age 46
RAFAELA CAPO, his wife, daughter of Antº and of Rafaela Fabregas, age 40
CATALINA, their daughter, age 13
RAFAELA, her sister, age 11
ANTᴬ, sister, age 8
MIGᴸ, son of the said Antº and his deceased wife Catalina Medina, age 20
    1 male slave, not baptized

1793: St. Augustine and North River

152.
PEDRO ANT⁰ RISO, son of Pedro and of Antª Castel, widower, age 46
JOSEF MENUCE, son of Marcos and of Magdalª Roque, age 46
JUANA RISO, his wife, daughter of Pedro and of Antª Castel, age 41
MARCOS, their son, age 8
JUANA, his sister, age 5
PEDRO, brother, age 3
JORJE, son of the said Juana and of her previous husband, age 18

153.
GABRIEL TRIAY, son of Ant° and of Ana Quintana, age 36
MARGARITA SANZ [PONS?], his wife, daughter of Estevan and of Magdalena Hernand^z, age 30
ANT°, their son age 11
GABRIEL, his brother, age 7
ANA, his sister, age 4

154.
ALBERTO ROQER, son of Ramon and of Catalina Lina, age 36
ANTᴬ VILLA, his wife, daughter of Fran^{co} and of Maria Ferrer, age 32
CATALINA, their daughter, age 9
RAMON, her brother, age 7
MARIA, her sister, age 3
    1 male slave, convert

[s.1-159]

155.
JUAN POMAR, son of Josef and of Juana Lina, age 26
MARIANA HERNAND^z, his wife, daughter of Jose and of Mariana Mir, age 18
JOSEF, their son, age 2

156.
JOSEF ARNAU, son of Josef and of Inez Girez, age 29
MAGDALENA MAUNUSI, his wife, daughter of Jose and of Juana Peis, age 14

157.
ANDRES LOPEZ, son of Andres and of Juana Triay, age 30
ANTᴬ GOMEZ, his wife, daughter of Martin and of Antª Triay, age 19
ANDRES, their age 4
JUANA, his sister, age 2

158.
MIG^L NAVARRO, son of Mig^l and of Rosa Rabel, age 36
MARIA TOMSON, his wife, daughter of Thomas and Maria Mongumrey, age 22

_____1793 : St. Augustine and North River

159.
BARTOLOMEO ALCINA, son of Bartolomeo and of Benita Pallecier, age 53
MARIA LUKE, his wife, daughter of Andres and of Margarita Bannuche, age 40
MARIA, their daughter, age 8
MARGARITA, her sister, age 5
ANTONIO, brother, age 4

[s.2-159]

160.
ANT° PONZ, son of Ant° and of Margarita Cardona, age 40
BENITA ALCINA, his wife, daughter of Bartolomeo and of Maria Lucas, age 19
MARGARITA, their daughter, age 4
MARIA, her sister, age 2

161.
PEDRO ESTOPA, son of Pedro and of Margarita Pallicer, age 43
ANA QUINTANA, his wife, daughter of Matheo and of Juana Caballero, age 56

162.
MIGUEL VILLALONGA, son of Mig^l and of Martina, daughter of the above
   [Pedro and Ana], age 37, widower
MARTINA, their daughter, age 12
AGUEDA, her sister, age 11
RAFAELA, her sister, age 8
FRAN^{CA}, sister, age 6
CATALINA, sister, age 3

1st: Cross Street

163.
BARNEY OGDEN, son of Moyses and of Maria Cousons, age 37, Protestant

164.
BARTOLOME FIGUERA, son of Mig^l and of Juana Pomar, age 44
JUANA ARNAU, his wife, daughter of Diego and of Juana Vicarias, age 42
MIGUEL, their son, age 15, single
DIEGO, his brother, age 12
JUANA, sister, age 8
BARTOLOME, brother, age 3

1793: St. Augustine and North River

165.
JORJE CLA, son of Jorje and of Maria Pritos, age 36
INEZ PURLA, his wife, daughter of Pedro and of Marianna Rodrig^z, age 43

[s.1-160]

GEORJE, their son, age 7
PEDRO DURAN, son of Pedro, the first husband of the said Inez, age 18
ANDRES BROWN, son of Andres, the second husband of the said Inez, age 10

166.
DIEGO HERNANDEZ, son of Diego and of Michaela Lesana, age 63
VICTORIA VIVAS, his wife, daughter of Ant° and of Agueda Villa, age 52

167.
MANUEL SUAREZ, son of Fran^{co} and of Rosa de Lias, age 27
AGUEDA HERNAND^z, his wife, daughter of Diego and Victoria Vivas, age 18

168.
ANT^A CLA, daughter of Jorje and of Maria Pretos, age 61

169.
JOSEF HERNANDEZ, son of Josey and of Magdalena Cardona, age 46
JUANA LINA, his wife, daughter of Juan and of Juana Acosta, age 53

170.
ANT° ANDREU, son of Juan and of Angela Caulas, age 42
AGUEDA PONZ, his wife, daughter of Pedro and Magdalena Pallicer, age 37
JUAN, their son, age 19, single
ANT°, his brother, age 13
MAGDALENA, sister, age 8
JUANA [PONZ], sister of the said Agueda, age 29, living with them

171.
JOSEF HERNAND^z, son of Jose and of Martina Victoria, age 45
MARIA MIR, his wife, daughter of Gabriel and of Catalina Pom, age 32
CATALINA, their daughter, age 13
JOSEF, her brother, age 10
MARIA ROSA, sister, age 8

[s.2-160]

GABRIEL, brother, age 6
DIEGO, brother, age 4
JUAN, brother, age 2

1793 : St. Augustine and North River

172.
PEDRO OSIAS, son of Geronimo and Ana Christiana [*no surname*], age 40
MARIA ORTEGAS, his wife, daughter of Sebastian Cherez [Chenez], age 32
  PEDRO, their son, age 11
  ANA, his sister, age 8
  SEBASTIAN, brother, age 5
  MARIA, sister, age 2

173.
PEDRO SABATE, son of Mig^l and of Catalina Capo, age 33
ANT^a HORTEGAS, his wife, daughter of Sebastian and of Ana Chenez, age 28
  MIG^l, their son, age 9
  CATALINA, his sister, age 7
  ANA, sister, age 5
  SEBASTIAN, brother, age 2
  1 female slave, convert
ANA CHEREZ, daughter of Lorenzo and of Maria Hernand^z, widow, age 61

174.
LUIS TRUTILON, son of Josef and of Maria Ana Vidata, age 29
JUANA GOMEZ, his wife, daughter of Martin and of Ant^a Tudoni, age 16
ANT^a TUDONI, daughter of Agustin and of Juana Triay, widow, age 47

175
PEDRO HULL, son of Juan and of Margarita Ferrer, age 42
MARIA ISABEL MORLAN, his wife, daughter of Fran^{co} and Maria Crosby, age 28
MARIA WATSON, daughter of Pedro and of said Maria, age 8
  1 female slave, baptized

176.
FRAN^{co} DALMEDO, son of Juan and of Juana Manent, age 41
[s.1–161]
JUANA VENZ, his wife, daughter of Pedro and Ana Ferrer [Ferren?], age 30
ANA MARIA, their daughter, age 6
JOSEF, her brother, age 1

177.
SEBASTIAN COLL, son of Sebastian and of Fran^{ca} Ponz, age 35
MARGARITA VILLA, his wife, daughter of Pedro and of Ant^a Fiol, age 30
  SEBASTIAN, their son, age 11
  PEDRO COLL, his brother, age 7
  JOSEF COLL, his brother, age 2
  1 female slave, convert

1793: St. Augustine and North River

178.
MIGUEL SEGUI, son of Nicolas and of Magdalena Campino, age 39
MAGDALENA, his daughter, age 18
JUANA, her sister, age 13
NICOLAS, brother, age 10
GUILLERMO, brother, age 5

179.
JOSEF BULCHANY, son of Mig.l and Felicia Marialy, age 44
MARIA ACOSTA, his wife, daughter of Domingo and Maria Bross, age 32
ROSA MARIA, their daughter, age 5
ANT.A DE LA CRUX, her sister, age 1
MIG.L MACLORIDE, son of said Maria and another husband, age 13

180.
NICOLAS NICOLICHE, son of Martin and Maria Tarrabuche, age 46
JOSEFA COLL, his wife, daughter of Bartolom.e and Josefa Ponz, age 36
MANAN, their son, age 9
MARIA, his sister, age 5
RAFAELA, sister, age 2
MANUELA, sister, age 7 months

[s.2-161]

181.
MARTIN MAREDEN, son of Edwardo and Inez Mureden, age 41
SERAH NELSON, his wife, daughter of Reason and of Hana Wilson, his wife, age 27, Protestant
ANA, their daughter, age 5
JUAN, her brother, age 4
MARIA ANA, brother, age 2

2nd Cross Street

182.
JOSE TURDAS, son of Thomas and Geronima Jacome, age 30
MARIA MAGDALENA GAVARDY, his wife, daughter of Ant.o and of Catalina Olibera, age 22
GERONIMA, their daughter, age 5
THOMAS, her brother, age 4 months
4 slaves, converts

_____ 1793 : St. Augustine and North River

183.
D^N MANUEL DE ALMANZA, son of D^n Fran^co and of D^a Josefa de Troya y
   Reguera, age 48
D^A LUISA PEREZ, his wife, daughter of D^n Bartolomeo and of D^a Beatriz de
   la Rosa, age 39
JUAN ANT°, their son, age 13
FELICITA JOSEFA, his sister, age 11
ANT^A, sister, age 9
PAULA, sister, age 6
            3 slaves, converts

184.
PEDRO TRIAY, son of Mig^l and of Ana Triay, age 39
MARIA ALBERTY, his wife, daughter of Ant° and [no given name] Slop, age 18
MIGUEL, their son, age 3
ANA FRAN, daughter of Isabel [sic] Eundori and of Fran^ca, widow, age 63
MARIA PEREGRINO, daughter of Matheo and of Ana Maria Triay, age 81

3rd Cross Street
[s.1-162]

185.
JUAN JOANEDA, son of Ant° and Margarita Morida, widower, age 37

186.
EDWARDO ASTON, son of Samuel and of Margarita Adeur, age 46
MARIA HINDSMAN, his wife, daughter of Ant° and Barbara Shasburgh, age 37 [?]
GUILLERMO, son, age 6
MARIA, his sister, age 5
JUANA, sister, age 4
PHELIPE ASTON, son of the above Eduardo and another wife, age 19, single
EDWARDO, brother, age 14
ISABEL MOT, daughter of the above Hindsman and another husband, single,
   age 18
ANA, her sister, age 16, single
MARGARITA HINDSMAN, daughter of Antonio and Barbara Mhasburgh [sic],
   single, age 29

101

1793: St. Augustine and North River

187.

D[N] JULIAN DE SALAS, son of Juan and of Juana Sanchez, age 29
D^ TERESA DE JESUS RODRIG^z^, his wife, daughter of D^n^ Lorenzo and of D^a^ Isabel Prima, age 17
JUAN PABLO MANUEL, son, age 1 month
JUAN PONZ, son of Juan and Margarita Rodavers, age 19, apprentice
JUAN FERDAND^z^, son of Santiago and of Ramona Solano, age 16, apprentice

4th Cross Street

188.

D^N^ RAFAEL ESPINOSA SAHABEDRA, son of Tomas and of Agustina Espinosa de los Monituros, age 31
D^A^ MARIA GONZALES, his wife, daughter of Christostimo and of Juana Montes de Oca, age 31
THOMAS, their son, age 5

[s.2–162]

ROBERTO, his brother, age 3
AGUSTINA MARIA ROSA, his sister, age 1
ANT° GONZALES, brother of the said Maria, age 12
LEONARDA, his sister, age 1
1 female slave, convert

5th Cross Street

189.

D^N^ DIMAS CORTES, son of Ant° and D^a^ Sebastiana Quesada, age 36
D^A^ AGUEDA SEGUI, his wife, daughter of D^[n]^ Bernardo and of D^a^ Agueda Villalonga, age 18
CLAUDIO, son, age 8 months

190.

MARGARITA OLARD, free mulatto, convert
MARIA, her daughter, age 8
JUAN, brother of Maria, age 6
MARGARITA ANASTACIA, sister, age 2 months
JUAN SMITH, mulatto, living with them, Protestant

_____1793 : St. Augustine and North River

6ᵗʰ Cross Street

191.
ANTº GUERTAS, son of Arimes and of Luisa Rupir, age 41
CATALINA AGUILAR, his wife, daughter of Juan and of Melchoria Ramos, age 22
JUAN ANTº, their son, age 3
AGUEDA DOROTEA, his sister, age 1
CATALINA JONES, English, Protestant [*no age*]

192. [part of above household]
GASPAR PAPI, son of [blank]
WILLIBY PUE, son of Luiz and of Margarita Pue, widower, age 50, Protestant

193.
D[ᴺ] ROQUE LEONARDY, son Jacoba Beag—one [*portion illegible*], age 59
D[ᴬ] AGUEDA COLL, his wife, daughter of Bartolomeo and of Josefa Ponz, age 41
[s.1-163]
CLORINDA JOSEFA, their daughter, single, age 17
JUAN, her brother, [no age]
BARTOLOMEO, brother, age 9
JACOBA, sister, age 6
MARGARITA, sister, age 3
    1 female slave, convert
    3 negro servants, 1 baptized

194.
Dᴺ MANUEL RENGIL, son of Don Mig^l and of Dᵃ Catalina Batuarte, age 28
Dᴬ MARIA JONES, his wife, daughter of Indigo and Margarita Woodland, age 25
IGNACIO, their son, age 6 months

7ᵗʰ Cross Street

195.
JUAN SUAREZ, son of Bartolome and of Isabel Navarro, age 45
JUANA MARTIN, his wife, daughter of Bartolome and of Maria Suarez, age 45
GREGORIO, son, age 18, single
JOSEF, his brother, age 15

1793: St. Augustine and North River

196.
D^N MARTIN MARTINEZ, son of Gregorio and of Isabel Soriano, age 34
LUCIA CORUNA, his wife, daughter of Josef and of Manuela Garcia, age 15
RITA MARIA, daughter, age 1

197.
D[N] JUAN SAUNDERS, Protestant
3 sons
                  19 slaves, none baptized

8th [Street] Market Road

198.
JOSEF ANT° CORUNA, son of Pedro and of Ursula Suarez, age 47
JOSEFA GARCIA, his wife, daughter of Juan and of Lucia Sanchez, age 44
ANT°, their son, age 24, single

199.
PEDRO ACOSTA, son of Josef and of Maria Rodrig^z, age 44
CECILIA ARTILES, his wife, daughter of Juan and of Josefa Sardina, age 43
                                                              [s.2-163]
JOSEFA, daughter, age 12
MARIA, her sister, age 10
LUIS, brother, age 8
THOMOSA, sister, age 5
CATALINA, sister, age 2

_____ 1793 : St. Augustine and North River

Banks of the Matanzas River

200.
JUAN FERRER, son of Josef and of Juana Flucha, age 37
JUANA HOCHA [FLUCHA?], his wife, daughter of Josef and of Margarita Losano, age 43

201.
FERNANDO FELANY, son of Santiago [*no age given*]
MARGARITA BELORY, his wife [*no age given*]
SANTIAGO, son, age 13
TERESA, his sister, age 7
MARGARITA, sister, age 5

202.
FRAN^{co} PALLICER, son of Ant° and of Juana Cintas [Lintas?], age 39
JUANA BILLA [VILLA], his wife, daughter of Fran^{co} and of Maria Ferrer, age 28
MARIA, their daughter, age 9
ANT^A, her sister, age 6
FRAN^{co}, brother, age 4
JUAN ANT°, infant of 6 months
CATALINA FEMENIAS, age 18, single
    3 slaves, not baptized

203.
JOSEF DUPONT, son of Abraham and of Juana Isabel Dupree, age 50, Protestant
ANA DUPONT, his wife, daughter of D^n Gideon and of D^a Ana Goodbee, age 48, Protestant
ABRAHAM, their son, age 25, single, Protestant
GUEIDO, his brother, age 21, single, Protestant
ANA, sister, age 23, single, Protestant
JUANA ISABEL, sister, age 18, single, Protestant

[s.1-164]

MARIA MAGDALENA, sister, age 16, single, Protestant
ISABEL GOODBEE, sister, age 14, Protestant
REBECCA, sister, age 4
    28 slaves, not baptized

1793: St. Augustine and North River

204.
HEPUORTH CARTER, son of Thomas and of Maria Hepuorth, age 43, Protestant
MARGARITA M^cLEAN, his wife, daughter of Juan and Isabel Page, age 39, Protestant
ISABEL, their daughter, age 15, Protestant
MARIA, her sister, age 12, Protestant
MARGARITA MARIA, sister, age 5
THOMAS MAN^L, brother, age 2
     25 slaves, not baptized

205.
SANTIAGO BARNEBY, son of Juan and Susana Diegos, age 37, Protestant
ANA GOLD, his wife, age 26, Protestant
SUSANAH BARNEBY, their daughter, age 10
ANA, her sister, age 8
MARIA, sister, age 2
     1 male slave, not baptized

206.
JUAN HOLZENDORF, son of Federico and of Rosina Dupont, 40, Protestant
ISABEL ERHARDT, his wife, daughter of Fran^{co} and of Maria Urbino —ollett [illegible], age 36, Protestant
JUAN LUIS REAL, son, age 17, single, Protestant
GUILLERMO BLUNTON, brother, age 10, Protestant
ISABEL ROSINA, sister, age 2
     1 female slave, not baptized

_____1793 : St. Augustine and North River

Banks of the North River

207.
JUAN XIMENEZ, widower, age 60

208.
ANASTACIO MABRUMATE, son of Ant° and of Maria Marculina, widower, age 56
ANT°, son of [above] and of his deceased wife Fran^{ca} Llabres, age 15
MARIA, daughter, age 11

[s.2-164]

CATALINA, sister, age 8
MARGARITA, sister, age 6
MARIANA, sister, age 3
                1 male slave, not baptized

209.
PEDRO FUCHIA, son of Josef and of Margarita Llesano, age 42
FRAN^{CA} PRETOS, his wife, daughter of Santiago and Fran^{ca} [no surname], age 38

210.
JUAN SEGUI, son of Benito and of Magdalena Peluda, age 37
AGUEDA HENRIQUE, his wife, daughter of Mateo and of Juana Pallicer, age 26
BENITO, their son, age 8
MARGARITA, his sister, age 4

211.
BERNARDO HERNAU [ARNAU], son of Martin and of Maria Mula, age 42
MARIA SANZ, his wife, daughter of Cosme and of Maria Mula [sic], age 37
MARTIN ARNAU, son of above, age 4
PEDRO LAMIRA, son of Guillermo and of the above Maria, age 10

212.
DOMINGO SEGUI, son of Domingo and of Ant^a, widower, age 36
DOMINGO, son of the above and of his deceased wife, age 9

213.
THOMAS ANDREU, son of Juan Andreu and of Angela Caulas, age 31
MARGARITA PREITES, his wife, daughter of Jaime and of Fran^{ca} Pietos, age 31
JUAN, their son, age 11
FRANCISCA, his sister, age 7
JAIME, brother, age 5
MARGARITA, sister, age 3

1793: St. Augustine and North River

214.
D[n] FRAN[co] SANCHEZ, son of D[n] Josef and of D[a] Juana Perez, age 56
D[a] MARIA DEL CARMEN HILL, his wife, daughter of Teophilo and of Teresa Tomas, age 23

[s.1-165]

RAFAELA, their daughter, age 5
MANUEL, her brother, age 3
FRAN[co], brother, age 1
    59 slaves, 9 baptized

215.
GUILLERMO SMITH, son of Thomas and of Catalina, age 38
ANA DAWRINO[?], his wife, daughter of Patricio and of Ana Farrell, age 26
JUAN, their son, age 5

216.
ANT[o] HINDSMANS, son of Ant[o] and of Barbara Mrasbourgh, age 43
ELONORA GENOBLE, his wife, daughter of Juan and of Ana, age 28
MARIA BARBARA, their daughter, age 7
CATALINA ANT[a], her sister, age 5
LUCIA, her sister, age 2
    1 slave, not baptized

217.
JUAN SALOM, son of Mig[l] and of Juana Ponz, age 40
MARGARITA NIELO, his wife, daughter of Juan and of Clara Victorina, age 36
JUAN, son, age 13
CLARA, sister, age 10
MARGARITA, her sister, age 5
MIGUEL, her brother, age 3
JUANA, sister, age 1

218.
D[n] MANUEL MARSHAL MALTER, age 49
D[a] TERESA TOMAS, his wife, daughter of Juan and of Christina, age 49
ALEXANDRO, son of Manuel and of previous wife Maria Douglas, age 16, single
CHRISTINA HILL, daughter of Teresa and previous husband Teophilo, age 18
MARIA [HILL], her sister, age 14
ISABEL [HILL], sister, age 12
ANA, sister, age 6
JUAN, sister, age 6
    12 slaves, none baptized

[s.2-165]

1793 : St. Augustine and North River

219.
ROBERTO ANDREUS, overseer of Don Franco Sanchez, age 41, Protestant
ANA JEMISON, his wife, age 38, Protestant
ANA, daughter, age 7

220.
JUAN FATIO, Protestant, single, age 35
16 negroes, property of Dª Maria Guanz, 6 baptized

221.
PEDRO MAESTRE, son of Bartolome and of Antª [no surname], age 45
MARIA ANDREU, his wife, daughter of Juan and of Angela Caulas, age 36
BARTOLOME, their son, age 19
JUAN, brother, age 14
ANGELA, sister, age 7
ANTᴬ, sister, age 5
PEDRO, brother, age 3

222.
JUAN CAPO, son of Gabriel and of Antª Mesguilson [?], age 53
AGUEDA SEGUI, his wife, daughter of Migl and of Maria Olibas, age 52
PEDRO, son of the above Juan and of Esperania Mall, single, age 19
JUAN, son of the above Juan and of Maria Cintos, age 13
GABRIEL, his brother, age 10
3 slaves, 1 baptized

223.
LAZARO ORTEGAS, son of Ignacio and of Ana, age 35
CATALINA LLEBRES, his wife, daughter of Jaime and of Catalina, age 34
CATALINA, their daughter, age 12
FRANᶜᴬ, her sister, age 6
IGNACIO HORTEGAS, son of Lazaro and of Franca Nand, widower, age 54

[s.1-166]

224.
LORENZO CAPELLA, son of Mateo and of Jeronima Suau [sic], age 30
CATALINA DURAN, his wife, daughter of Pedro and of Inez Paulo, age 23
GERONIMA, their daughter, age 7
MATHIAS, her brother, age 4

225.
JUAN ANDREU, son of Juan and of Angela Caulas, age 47
CATALINA PONZ, his wife, daughter of Migl and of Franca Coll, age 51

[continued on next page]

1793: St. Augustine and North River

225. (cont'd)

JUAN, their son, age 23, single
MIG^L, brother, age 22, single
ANT°, brother, age 17, single
FRAN^{CA}, sister, age 14, single
FRAN^{CA}, another sister, age 6
CATALINA, sister, age 4

226.

D^N AGUSTIN BOYKE, son of Dr Pedro and D^a Maria Catalina [*no surname*], age 27
8 slaves, none baptized

NOTE: The batallion that garrisons this
place is composed of: 346 men
the small party of artillery: 23 men
the dragoons: 17 men
convicts: 52

1813

Census of St. Augustine, St. John's, and Fernandina

Church District: St. Augustine

Translator's note:

The original document contains no lines, breaks, or other divisions between households. For readability, breaks are added below at points that appear to be "natural" divisions. However, the possibility remains that any two or more adjacent groupings may have occupied the same household, considering the prevailing housing pattern in which persons did reside within non-nuclear family units.

[s. 2–213

Name	Age
D^N ANTONIO HUERTAS	53
D^A CATALINA AGUILAR, his wife	40
2 sons	1–7
4 daughters	10–20
2 daughter	7–14
4 male slaves	15–25
FRAN^co PAZ, living with them	35
D^N GASPAR PAPY	61
D^N ANA PONS his wife	49
3 sons	15–25
2 daughters	18–20
4 slaves	15–25
1 slave	1–7

Source location: sheets 1–213 through 1–216 and 1–208/83 through 2–209/207. Of the two and three sets of numbers used, the first represents the side of the page, the second is the stamped sheet number, and the third is the penned sheet number.

1813: St. Augustine, St. John's, and Fernandina

D^N JOSE ARGUELLES, absent	35
D^A LUISA CANTO, his wife	32
3 sons	7-14
3 daughters	8-16
1 female slave	15-25
1 female slave	1-7
D^A MELCHORA RAMOS	70
D^A FRAN^{CA} DE AGUILAR, widow	42
2 sons	15-25
2 sons	7-14
1 daughter	1-7
1 female associate living with them	7-18
5 male slaves	15-25
2 male slaves	5-15
D^N BART^{ME} DE CASTRO Y FERRER	54
D^A ANTONIA SEGUI, his wife	37
10 male slaves	25-35
10 male slaves	1-7
15 female slaves	15-35
15 female slaves	1-14

[s.1–214]

D^N FERNANDO ARREDONDO, absent	55
D^A BRIGIDA GOMEZ, his wife	41
1 son	7-15
4 daughters	15-25
1 daughter	7-14
2 daughters	1-7
2 male slaves	15-25
D^N PEDRO MIRANDO	45
D^A MARIA SANCHEZ, his wife	29
1 son	1-5
3 daughters	7-14
4 male slaves	15-25
2 male slaves	1-7

1813: St. Augustine, St. John's, and Fernandina

D^N GIL PICOT, Cap^n of Cuba	65
D^A FLORA CELIA, his wife	60
1 daughter	15-25
1 female slave	25-30
JUAN ARNAU	60
ISABEL FERRER his wife	60
D^A AGUEDA VILLALONGA, widow	61
2 daughters	15-25
7 male slaves	15-25
3 female slaves	25-35
D^N BERN^{DO} SEGUI	29
D^A DIONISIA RODRIG^Z, his wife	25
2 sons	1-7
1 male slave	7-15
2 male slaves	7-25 [sic]
D^N EUSEBIO GOMEZ	31
D^A BLANCA SEGUI, his wife	31
1 son	1-7
3 daughters	1-5
D^N JOSE REYES	28
D^A MARIA SEGUI, his wife	27
1 son	1-5
1 daughter	1-3
	[s.2-214]
D^N JUAN HUERTAS	24
D^A CIRILIA GUADORROMA, his wife	20
3 male slaves	7-14
D^N FELIPE SOLANA	30
D^A CATALINA PAPY, his wife	27
4 sons	1-7
3 male slaves	15-27
D^N JOSE M^A UGARTE	37
D^A MARIA LEONARDY, his wife	24
3 sons	1-7
4 male slaves	20-30

1813: St. Augustine, St. John's, and Fernandina

D^N FRAN^{CO} PELLICER	60
D^A JUANA VILA, his wife	49
3 sons	15-25
2 sons	7-7 [sic]
3 daughters	7-14
1 female associate living with them	15-20
9 male slaves	15-25
D^N DOMINGO REYES	64
1 son	15-25
1 daughter	15-25
D^N DOMINGO REYES, the younger	30
D^A MARIA PAPY, his wife	25
2 daughters	1-7
AGUSTIN ISERN, sergeant of Cuba	50
ISABEL MESTRE, his wife	23
4 sons	1-7
D^N RAMON DE FUENTES	59
D^A MARIA PERRY, his wife	40
4 sons	15-25
2 daughters	1-7
4 daughters	10-15
2 female slaves	15-25

[s.1–215]

D^N MANUEL SOLANA	75
D^A MARIA MESTRE, his wife	50
2 sons	15-25
2 sons	7-15
2 daughters	15-20
10 male slaves	15-25
D^N RAMON CASTILLO, lieutenant of Cuba	60
D^A CATALINA HOTA[?], his wife	35
2 sons	2-7
D^N JUAN ANDREU	45
D^A MARIA MABRUMATY, his wife	36
3 sons	7-14
3 sons	1-7
5 male slaves	15-25
2 male slaves	7-14

1813: St. Augustine, St. John's, and Fernandina

D^N JUAN FERNANDEZ	36
6 male slaves	15-25
CARLOS DOMINGUEZ	33
MARIA MURO, his wife	36
2 sons	5-10
D^N JUAN LEONARDY	35
D^A CATALINA ROGERO, his wife	30
3 sons	7-14
JUAN BAUT^{TA} COLLINS, free *pardo*	60
1 son	7-15
D^N JOSE FONTANEL	60
D^A MARIA HOUSTON [ASHTON], his wife	36
3 sons	15-25
2 sons	1-7
1 son	5-15
7 slaves	15-25
FRAN^{CO} ESTACHOLY	65
MARIA LEGAS, his wife	65
2 male slaves	7-14

[s.2–215]

D^N CRISTOBAL BRABO, 2nd lieut. of Cuba	54
D^A JOSEFA LEGAS, his wife	35
2 sons	1-7
2 daughters	7-14
D^N FRAN^{CO} MEDICES	33
D^A ANTONIA PELLICER, his wife	27
4 sons	1-7
1 slave	7-14
LEON DUVIGNON, free *pardo*	35
his mate, free *morena* [*no name given*]	30
5 sons	7-14
D^N JOAQUIN SANCHEZ	50
D^A M^A RITA BRABO, his wife	40
6 sons	15-25
2 daughters	1-7

1813: St. Augustine, St. John's, and Fernandina

D^N FERD^{DO} DE LA MAZA ARREDONDO, the younger	26
D^A MARIANA ENTRALGO, his wife	26
3 sons	1-7
12 male slaves	15-25
6 male slaves	7-14
9 female slaves	15-25
7 female slaves	7-7 [sic]
D^N JOSE HERNANDEZ	25
D^A ANA HILL, his wife	25
2 sons	2-7
1 daughter	5-10
40 male slaves	15-25
32 female slaves	7-15
D^A CATALINA DE LOS IJUELOS [?], widow	53
1 son	15
2 daughters	15-25
2 slaves	15-25

[s.1–216]

DON JUAN BUSQUET	60
D^A JOSEFA BLANCA, his wife	50
6 male slaves	5-25
D^N FERD^{DO} DE LA PISENTE, capt., of Cuba	68
D^A LEONOR LOWE, his wife	49
3 slaves	15-25
JOSE FERNANDEZ	63
ANA SANCHEZ, his wife	38
3 sons	1-7
2 daughters	7-15
D^N MANUEL DEBEN	60
D^N ISAK WICKS	75
3 slaves	35-70

1813: St. Augustine, St. John's, and Fernandina

FELIPE EMBARA, free *moreno*	53
FELICIA SANCHEZ, his wife, free	50
2 sons	7-14
2 daughters	7-15
JUAN Bᵀ SANCHEZ	60
AGUEDA, his wife	61

1813: St. Augustine, St. John's, and Fernandina

1813 Census of the Residents of the Lower St. John's River

[s.2–208/83]

Whites	Negro Slaves
8 single males 0-7	26 single males 0-7
11 single females 0-7	29 single females 0-7
7 single males 7-16	38 single males 7-16
5 single females 7-16	24 single females 7-16
5 single male 16-25	42 single males 16-25
3 single females 16-25	35 single females 16-25
1 married male 16-25	43 single males 25-40
4 married females 16-25	40 single females 25-40
2 widowed females 16-25	11 single males 40-50
6 single males 15-40	8 single females 40-50
3 single females 25-40	12 single males over 50
6 married males 25-40	11 single females over 50
7 married females 25-40	
2 single males 40-50	
2 married males 40-50	
1 married female 40-50	
1 single female over 50	
3 married males over 50	
2 widowed females over 50	

Totals:
1 June 1813

Whites 79
Slaves 319

1813: St. Augustine, St. John's, and Fernandina

1813 Census of Residents of the Upper St. John's River

[s.2-209/85]

Whites			Free Mulattos		
7 single	males	0-7	3 single	females	0-7
2 single	males	0-7	3 single	females	0-7
5 single	females	0-5	4 single	males	7-16
5 single	males	7-16	1 single	male	25-40
3 single	females	7-16	1 single	female	25-40
4 single	males	16-25			
1 single	female	16-25			
10 single	males	25-40			
9 married	males	25-40			
10 married	females	25-40			
1 single	male	40-50			
2 married	males	40-50			
2 married	females	40-50			
2 married	males	over 50			
1 married	female	over 50			
3 widowed	males	over 50			

[continued on next page]

1813: St. Augustine, St. John's, and Fernandina

[Upper St. John's, cont'd]

Free Negroes	Negro Slaves
1 single female 25-40	5 single males 0-7
	5 single females 0-7
	4 single males 7-16
	4 single females 7-16
	3 single males 16-25
	6 single females 16-25
	15 single males 25-40
	2 single females 25-40
	4 single males 40-50
	6 single females 40-50
	2 single males over 50

Totals:
1 June 1813

Whites	65
Free Mulatto	11
Free Negroes	1
Negro Slaves	56

1813: St. Augustine, St. John's, and Fernandina

Census of the Residents of the Section of Fernandina

[s.2–210]

Whites			
57	single	males	0-7
61	single	females	0-7
31	single	males	7-16
36	single	females	7-16
25	single	males	16-25
17	single	females	16-25
2	married	males	16-25
26	married	females	16-25
2	widowed	males	16-25
1	widowed	female	16-25
17	single	males	25-40
1	single	male	25-40
45	married	males	25-40
35	married	females	25-40
2	widowed	males	25-40
4	widowed	females	25-40
2	single	males	40-50
1	single	female	40-50
13	married	males	40-50
11	married	females	40-50
2	widowed	males	40-50
3	widowed	females	40-50
2	single	males	over 50
1	single	female	over 50
15	married	males	over 50
6	married	females	over 50
4	widowed	males	over 50
1	widowed	female	over 50

Free Mulattos			
3	single	males	0-7
4	single	females	0-7
6	single	males	7-16
1	single	female	7-16
2	single	males	16-25
3	single	females	16-25
3	single	males	25-40
1	single	female	25-40
1	single	male	40-50
1	widowed	female	40-50
1	widowed	female	over 50

Free Negroes			
4	single	males	16-25
2	single	females	16-25
2	single	males	25-40
5	single	females	25-40
1	single	male	25-40
1	single	female	25-40

[continued on next page]

1813: St. Augustine, St. John's, and Fernandina

[Fernandina, cont'd]

Negro Slaves

97	single	males	0-7
58	single	females	0-7
77	single	males	7-16
52	single	females	7-16
109	single	males	16-25
72	single	females	16-25
1	married	male	16-25
1	married	female	16-25
1	widowed	female	16-25
167	single	males	25-40
112	single	females	25-40
56	single	males	40-50
21	single	females	40-50
2	married	males	40-50
2	married	females	40-50

Mulatto Slaves

5	single	males	0-7
4	single	females	0-7
4	single	males	7-16
2	single	female	7-16
6	single	females	16-25
1	single	male	25-40
1	single	female	25-40

Totals:
1 June 1813

Whites	428
Free Mulatto	26
Mulatto Slaves	23
Free Negroes	15
Negro Slaves	838

1814

Census outside St. Augustine
including
Mosquito Territory and Fernandina

Part 1: Mosquito Territory

"Statement that shows the inhabitants of the territory, their ages, children, slaves and those living with them, white and black—by order of the governor."

[s. 2–217 /101]

Name	Age
Dᴺ JUAN BUNCH	68
his wife	62
15 female slaves	20–60
8 female slaves	20–50
6 negro children	1–6
Dᴺ JUAN ADDISON	50
his wife	40
21 male slaves	20–60
13 female slaves	20–40
22 negro children	1–10
Dᴺ ROBTᴼ Mᶜʜᴀʀᴅʏ	40
his wife	22
5 male slaves	20–60
10 female slaves	20–50
13 negro children	1–9

Source location: sheets 2–217 /101 through 2–240 /147. Of the two triple-digit numbers for each sheet, the first is the stamped number and the second is penned.

1814: Outside St. Augustine

D^N JOSEF HERNANDEZ	26
his wife	25
3 sons	3–9
1 daughter	8
18 male slaves	20–60
15 female slaves	20–50
28 negro chidren	1–9
D^A R. ORMAND	50
her son	13
9 male slaves	20–60
12 female slaves	20–50
14 negro children	1–9
D^A FRAN^{CA} KERR	60
9 male slaves	20–50
9 female slaves	20–40
12 negro children	1–10
D^N GABRIEL G. PERPALL	47
18 male slaves	20–60
11 female slaves	20–50
20 negro children	1–12
GUILLERMO FLETCHER	60
JESSE HESTER	60
his wife	50
JESSE SULIVAN	40
FELIPE WIEDMAN	40
his wife	30
DANIEL SWEENY	30

St Agustin de la Florida
April 14, 1814
Gabriel G. Perpall

1814: Outside St. Augustine

Part 1 [A]: Mosquito Territory*

"Statement that shows the inhabitants of the territory, their ages, children, slave males and slave females, and all others living with them (white and colored), as by order of Senor Governor."

[s. 2-218 /103]

Name	Age
D^N JUAN BUNCH	68
D^A C. BUNCH his wife	62
15 male slaves	20–60
8 female slaves	20–50
6 negro children	1–6
D^N JUAN ADDISON	50
his wife	40
21 male slaves	20–50
13 female slaves	20–40
22 negro children	1–10
D^N ROBERTO M^CHARDY	40
his wife	22
5 male negroes	20–60
10 female negroes	20–50
13 negro children	1–9
D^N JOSE HERNANDEZ	26
his wife	25
4 children	3–8
18 male slaves	20–60
15 female slaves	20–50
28 negro children	1–9

Translator's note: This is a second draft of the preceding census. Some variations exist in the data.

1814: Outside St. Augustine

Dᴬ R. ORMAND	50
MANᴸ, her son	12
9 male slaves	20-60
12 female slaves	20-50
14 negro children	1-9
Dᴬ FRANᶜᴬ KERR	60
9 male slaves	20-50
9 female slave	20-40
12 negro children	1-10
Dᴺ GABᴸ G. PERPALL	47
his wife	24
2 sons	5-7
3 daughters	1-11
18 male slaves	20-60
11 female slaves	20-50
20 negro children	1-10
GUILLERMO FLETCHER	60
JESSE HESTER	60
his wife	50
JESSE SULIVAN	40
FELIPE WIEDMAN	38
his wife	30
SWENNY [*no first name given*]	30

Sᵗ Agustin de la Florida
April 14, 1814
Gabriel G. Perpall

1814: Outside St. Augustine

Part 2: St. Johns River

"Name census of the inhabitants of St. Johns River, with statements of the number in their families, those living with them, and servants."

[s.2–219 /105]

Name	Age	Free	Slave
ENRIQUE SWINEY	35	2	
his wife	31		
JUAN JONES, single	38	1	
RIBECA RICHARD, widow	25	4	1
1 daughter	0-7		
2 daughters	7-16		
1 female slave	7-16		
SAMUEL MILLER, widower	40	4	15
1 son	7-16		
1 daughter	0-7		
2 daughters	7-16		
1 male slave	0-7		
2 male slaves	7-16		
4 male slaves	16-25		
2 female slaves	0-7		
3 female slaves	7-16		
3 female slaves	16-25		
REBECCA HENDRICKS, widow	70	1	6
1 male slave	0-7		
1 male slave	7-16		
2 male slaves	16-25		
1 female slave	16-25		
1 female slave	25-40		

1814: Outside St. Augustine

ISSAC HENDRICKS	42	2	4
his wife	36		
1 male slave	0-7		
1 male slave	25-40		
2 female slaves	16-25		
GUILLERMO HARTLEY	24	2	1
his wife	20		
1 male slave	16-25		
ENRIQUE HARTLEY	28	2	
his wife	21		
EDWARD WANTON, single	45	1	9
2 male slaves	0-7		
2 male slaves	7-16		
1 male slave	16-25		
1 female slave	0-7		
3 female slaves	7-16		
JUAN BEARDING	28	2	
his wife	25		

[s.1–220 /107]

ELIJAH CHRISTIE	40	2	
his wife	33		
JONATHAN M^cCULLOCH, single	58	1	
ZAPHARIAH KINGSLEY, single	44	1	21
2 male slaves	0-7		
2 male slaves	7-16		
3 male slaves	16-25		
6 male slaves	25-40		
1 female slave	0-7		
3 female slaves	7-16		
4 female slaves	25-40		
JOSE SUMMERALL, widower	56	1	

1814: Outside St. Augustine

SARAH SUMMERAL, widow	30	1	5
1 male slave	16-25		
1 female slave	0-7		
2 female slaves	16-25		
1 female slave	25-40		
FRANCISCO HARTLEY, widower	63	1	
GUILLERMO GARDNER, single	32	1	
GUILLERMO BEARDING	32	3	
his wife	19		
1 son	0-7		
JUAN PETTY, widower	33	3	
1 son	0-7		
1 daughter	7-16		
ESABELA ASHTON, widow	46	3	
1 son	16-25		
1 daughter	16-25		
MOSES BOWDEN	29	2	
his wife	26		
AARON TRAVERS, single	41	1	
ROBERTO GILBERT	36	3	
his wife	25		
1 son	0-7		
JUAN GILBERT	32	2	
his wife	21		
SUSANA PLUMMER, widow	48	3	
1 son	16-25		
1 daughter	16-25		

[s.2–220 /108]

SARAH FAULKS, widow	36	4
1 son	7-16	
2 daughters	7-16	

1814: Outside St. Augustine

ROBERTO LOWING	50	2
his wife	46	
Total:	55	62

June 2, 1814
as agent for this purpose,
Jorje F. Clark

Part 3: St. Paul Channel

"Name Census of the inhabitants upon the St. Paul Channel, with statements of the number of their family members, those living with them, and their servants"

[s.2–221 /109]

Name	Age	Free	Slave
Plantation of Dⁿ JUAN FORBES,		2	119
overseer LINDSEY FOD, single	38		
overseer JORGE LATER, single	33		
18 male slaves	0-7		
16 male slaves	7-16		
13 male slaves	16-25		
4 male slaves	25-40		
11 male slaves	40-50		
9 male slaves	over 50		
12 female slaves	0-7		
8 female slaves	7-16		
5 female slaves	16-25		
12 female slaves	25-40		
5 female slaves	40-50		
6 female slaves	over 50		

1814: Outside St. Augustine

Plantation of Dᴺ BARTOLOME
DE CASTRE   1   40
overseer JUAN FRECY, single   32
 1 male slave   0-7
 3 male slaves   7-16
 2 male slaves   16-25
 3 male slaves   21-40
 9 male slaves   over50
 3 female slaves   0-7
 2 female slaves   7-16
 4 female slaves   16-25
 5 female slaves   25-40
 3 female slaves   40-50
 5 female slaves   over50

Plantation of Dᴺ JUAN FRASER   1   95
overseer JUAN WARDLOW, single   40
13 male slaves   7-16
24 male slaves   16-25
17 male slaves   25-40
 6 female slaves   7-16
17 female slaves   16-25
18 female slaves   25-40

Total: 4   254

June 2, 1813
as agent for the purpose,
Jorge F. Clarke

1814: Outside St. Augustine

Part 4: Talbot Island

"Name Census of the inhabitants of the Talbot Island, with statements of the number of their family members, those living with them, and servants."

[s.2–223 /113]

Name	Age	Free	Slave
JUAN HOUSTON, the father	58	5	10
his wife	55		
2 sons	7-16		
1 daughter	7-16		
1 male slave	0-7		
2 male slaves	7-16		
4 male slaves	25-40		
1 female slave	7-16		
2 female slaves	16-25		
JUAN HOUSTON, the son	26	2	11
his wife	19		
2 male slaves	0-7		
2 male slaves	7-16		
3 male slaves	16-25		
1 female slave	16-25		
3 female slaves	25-40		
LEWIS CHRISTOPHER	21[?]	2	12
his wife	17		
1 male slave	0-7		
1 male slave	7-16		
5 male slaves	16-25		
1 male slave	25-40		
1 female slave	7-16		
3 female slaves	25-40		
Total:		9	33

June 2, 1813
Jorje F. Clarke

1814: Outside St. Augustine

Part 5: St. Mary River

"Name Census of the inhabitants of St. Mary River, with statements of the family members, those living with them, and servants."

[s.1–224 /115]

Name	Age	Free	Slave
JUAN BRADDOCK	38	3	15
his wife	30		
1 son	0-7		
6 male slaves	25-40		
3 male slaves	40-50		
2 female slaves	0-7		
2 female slaves	7-16		
2 female slaves	25-40		
NATHANIEL WILDES	36	8	6 [sic]
his wife	30		
1 son	0-7		
1 daughter	0-7		
4 daughters	7-16		
2 male slaves	0-7		
3 male slaves	16-25		
1 male slave	25-40		
1 female slave	0-7		
3 female slaves	16-25		
ELIOZA[?] WATERMAN	45	7	15
his wife	35		
1 son	7-16		
1 daughter	0-7		
3 daughters	7-16		
2 male slaves	0-7		
1 male slave	7-16		
1 male slave	16-25		
3 male slaves	25-40		
2 male slaves	over 50		
3 female slaves	16-25		
3 female slaves	25-40		

1814: Outside St. Augustine

JUAN LOW	55	7	13
his wife	40		
2 sons	7-16		
1 son	25-40		
1 daughter	7-16		
1 daughter	16-25		
4 male slaves	0-7		
1 male slave	7-16		
2 male slaves	16-25		
3 male slaves	25-40		
1 female slave	0-7		
2 female slaves	16-25		
GUILLERMO CHRISTOPHER	32	4	20
his wife	26		
1 daughter	0-7		
1 daughter	7-16		
6 male slaves	0-7		
7 male slaves	16-25		
1 male slave	25-40		
2 female slaves	0-7		
4 female slaves	16-25		

[s.2–224 /116]

GUILLERMO BRADDOCK	35	4	14
his wife	30		
1 son	0-7		
1 daughter	7-16		
1 male slave	0-7		
7 male slaves	16-25		
1 female slave	0-7		
1 female slave	7-16		
4 female slaves	16-25		
SPICER CHRISTOPHER	26	2	17
his wife	22		
2 male slaves	0-7		
6 male slaves	25-40		
2 female slaves	0-7		
4 female slaves	16-25		
3 female slaves	25-40		

_____   1814: Outside St. Augustine

Total: 35   100

June 2, 1814
as agent for the purpose,
Jorge F. Clarke

Part 6: Tiger Island

"Name Census of the inhabitants of Tiger Island with statements of the number of their family members, those living with them, and servants."

[s.2–225 /117]

Name	Age	Free	Slave
GUILLERMO HALL	35	2	8
his wife	23		
1 male slave	16-25		
4 male slaves	25-40		
1 female slave	16-25		
2 female slaves	25-40		

June 2, 1814
as agent for the purpose,
Jorge F. Clarke

1814: Outside St. Augustine

Amelía Island

"Census of the inhabitants of Amelia Island, with statements of the numbers of their family members and those living with them, excluding Fernandina Port."

[s.1–226 /119]

Name	Age	Free	Slave
SAMUEL HARRISON	63	6	83
his wife	55		
1 son	7-16		
1 son	16-25		
1 daughter	7-16		
1 daughter	16-25		
5 male slaves	0-7		
6 male slaves	7-16		
6 male slaves	16-25		
20 male slaves	25-40		
20 male slaves	over 50		
5 female slaves	0-7		
5 female slaves	7-16		
4 female slaves	16-25		
2 female slaves	25-40		
10 female slaves	40-50		
ROBERTO HARRISON	35	2	2
his wife	23		
GUILLERMO SAUNDERS	32?	2	
his wife	22?		
ANTONIO SUAREZ	45	6	11
his wife	40		
1 son	7-16		
1 son	16-26		
2 daughters	16-26		
1 male slave	0-7		
3 male slaves	16-25		
4 male slaves	25-40		
1 female slave	0-7		
1 female slave	16-25		

1814: Outside St. Augustine

DOMINGO FERNANDEZ	46	3	20
his wife	38		
1 daughter	16-25		
1 male slave	0-7		
1 male slave	7-16		
8 male slaves	16-25		
3 male slaves	25-40		
3 female slaves	0-7		
1 female slave	7-16		
1 female slave	16-25		
2 female slaves	25-40		
LUCIA FITZGERALD, widow	55	2	28
tenant ISRIL POOL	36		
			[s.1–227 /120]
4 male slaves	0-7		
3 male slaves	7-16		
2 male slaves	16-25		
6 male slaves	25-40		
1 female slave	0-7		
5 female slaves	16-25		
7 female slaves	25-40		
FERDINAND M^cDONALD	40	6	12
his wife	31		
1 son	0-7		
2 sons	7-16		
1 daughter	0-7		
1 male slave	0-7		
1 male slave	16-25		
4 male slaves	25-40		
2 female slaves	7-16		
2 female slaves	16-25		
1 female slave	25-40		
1 female slave	over 50		
DIEGO PILOT, widower	60	1	14 [sic]
2 male slaves	0-7		
1 male slave	7-16		
5 male slaves	16-25		
1 male slave	40-50		
2 female slaves	0-7		
3 female slaves	25-40		

1814: Outside St. Augustine

JUAN VAUGHAN	45	3	10
his wife	40		
1 daughter	16-25		
1 male slave	0-7		
2 male slaves	7-16		
4 male slaves	25-40		
1 female slave	7-16		
2 female slaves	25-40		

June 2, 181
as agent for the purpose,
Jorge F. Clarke

Part 8: Nassau River

"Name Census of the Inhabitants of both Nassau Rivers, with a statement of the number of family members, those living with them, and servants."

[s.2–235 /137]*

Name	Age	Free	Slave
GUILLERMO FITZPATRICK	50	8	11
his wife	42		
1 son	0-7		
2 sons	7-16		
2 daughters	7-16		
1 daughter	16-25		
1 male slave	0-7		

[household continued on next page]

---

*Translator's note: Document pages 227 through 234 of this census series are repetitions of previous pages and are therefore not reproduced here.

1814: Outside St. Augustine

[Fitzpatrick, cont'd]

2 male slaves	7-16		
1 male slave	16-25		
2 female slaves	0-7		
2 female slaves	7-16		
2 female slaves	16-25		
1 female slaves	25-40		
DIEGO SMITH	40	5	32
his wife	32		
2 sons	7-16		
overseer JUAN LASSEE	36		
2 male slaves	0-7		
4 male slaves	7-16		
8 male slaves	16-25		
3 male slaves	25-40		
1 female slave	0-7		
6 female slaves	7-16		
6 female slaves	16-25		
2 female slaves	25-40		
JUAN EDWARDS, widower	58	4	13
1 son	0-7		
1 son	7-16		
1 daughter	7-16		
2 male slaves	7-16		
4 male slaves	16-25		
2 male slaves	25-40		
1 female slave	0-7		
2 female slaves	7-25		
2 female slaves	25-40		
CARLOS BREWER	28	3	3
his wife	26		
1 son	0-7		
2 male slaves	7-16		
1 male slave	16-25		
FRANCISCO BREWER	60	3	3 [*sic*]
his wife	44		
1 son	7-16		
3 male slaves	16-25		
1 female slave	16-25		
2 female slaves	25-40		

1814: Outside St. Augustine

[s.1–236 /138]

THOMAS LAMB	62	4	
his wife	46		
1 son	7-16		
1 daughter	7-16		
EZEKIAH TUCKER	38	7	
his wife	32		
1 son	0-7		
4 sons	7-16		
GUILLERMO HUGHBANK	31	2	2
his wife	28		
1 male slave	25-40		
1 male slave	40-50		
GUILLERMO STERRATS	30	2	10
his wife	21		
1 male slave	0-7		
1 male slave	7-16		
4 male slaves	16-25		
2 female slaves	16-25		
2 female slaves	25-40		
PEDRO MASSEY, single	26	1	5
3 male slaves	25-40		
2 female slaves	25-40		
Total:		39	79

June 2, 1814
as agent for the purpose,
Jorje F. Clarke

1814: Outside St. Augustine

Part 9: Fernandina on Amelia Island

"Name census of the residents that comprise the village of Fernandina on Amelia Island."

[s.2–236 /139]

Name	Age	Free	Slave
D^N PEDRO PONS	26	1	
D^A GETRUDIS CARRERAS, wife	23	1	
3 negro male slaves	14-30		3
living with them:			
D^A CLARA PACETY	42	1	
1 daughter	14-30	1	
D^N CARLOS CANTO	12	1	
D^N FELIPE ROBERTO YONGE	37	1	
D^A MARIA ATKINSON, wife	28	1	
2 sons	7-14	2	
25 negro male slaves	14-30		25
16 negro female slaves	14-30		16
living with them:			
D^N JOSE HIBBERSON	30	1	
D^N GUILLERMO LAWRENCE	39	1	
D^A ANA TRAVERS	30	1	
1 son	7-14	1	
1 daughter	14-30	1	
1 negro male slave	14-30		1
4 negro female slaves	14-30		4
living with them:			
D^A MARIA TRAVERS	21	1	
D^A MARGARITA TRAVERS	18	1	
D^N PEDRO CAPO	40	1	
D^A GERTRUDIS PACETY	30	1	
1 son	7-14	1	
2 daughters	7-14	2	
1 male slave	14-30		1
2 female slaves	14-30		2

1814: Outside St. Augustine

Dᴺ DOMINGO ESTACHOLY	41	1	
Dᴬ URSULA LLUFRIO, wife	29	1	
1 son	7-14	1	
1 female negro slave	14-30		1

[s.1–237 /140]

Dᴺ JUAN SOLANO	33	1	
CATALINA MIR, wife	30?	1	
1 son	7-14	1	
1 daughter	7-14	1	
1 negro slave	14-30		1

Dᴬ FRANCISCA ANDREU	35	1	
2 negro female slaves	14-30		2
living with them:			
Dᴬ FRANCISCA ANDREU	25	1	
2 sons	7-14	2	

Dᴺ JUAN MᶜCLURE	36	1	
4 male slaves	7-14		
8 male slaves	14-30		
6 male slaves	30-60		18
7 female slaves	14-13		7
living with them:			
Dᴺ JAYME ENGLISH	45	1	

Dᴺ JOSE ARNAU	60	1	
2 sons	14-30	2	
living with them:			
Dᴺ FRANCISCO TRIAY	30	1	
JUANA MANNEY, wife	25	1	

Dᴺ DAMION NAMIS	41	1	
Dᴬ JUANA LOPEZ, wife	28	1	
1 male slave	14-30		1
living with them:			
Dᴺ VICENTE VALENCIA	61	1	
1 son	7-14	1	

1814: Outside St. Augustine

GASPAR HERNANDEZ	51	1	
D^A MARGARITA ANDREU, wife	23	1	
living with them:			
D^N ANTONIO ANDREU	15	1	
D^N JOSE PEREZ	14	1	
D^A MARGARITA ROSY	45	1	
1 son	14-30	1	
1 daughter	7-14	1	
1 daughter	14-30	1	
1 male slave	14-30		1
living with them:			
D^A ANTONIA SANCHEZ	7	1	
D^N JOSE XIMENES	41	1	
living with him:			
D^A JUANA SEGUI	33	1	

[s.2–237 /141]

D^N JOSE ALVAREZ	43	1	
D^A JUANA BARBE, wife	20	1	
living with them:			
D^N MATEO TERRADAS	55	1	
D^N FRANCISCO BARBE	17	1	
1 male slave	30-60		1
D^N FELIX RENTEY	55	1	
living with him:			
D^A MARIA XIMENEZ	40	1	
1 son	14-30	1	
1 daughter	14-30	1	
D^N MIGUEL MABRITE	32	1	
D^A BARBARA ESTACHOLY, wife	29	1	
1 daughter	7-14	1	
living with them:			
D^N JUAN BUCHANY	22	1	
D^N ANTONIO DIAZ	25	1	
JOSE BERGALLO	36	1	
living with him:			
D^N JUAN LLAMA	36	1	

1814: Outside St. Augustine

Dⁿ JOSE CANDELARIA	40	1
JUANA SEGUI, his wife	34	1
3 sons	7-14	3
Dⁿ JAYME ARNAU	40	1
MARGARITA PASQUAL, wife		32	1
1 son	7-14	1
1 daughter	0-7	1
living with them:		
Dⁿ PEDRO PESO DE BURGO	40	1
1 daughter	7-14	1
Dⁿ JOSE OLMEDO	21	1
Dⁿ PEDRO ARNAU	22	1
Dⁿ GEORJE CLAR	28	1
Dⁿ JOSE GARRTET?	42	1
Dᵃ JUANA ATKINSON, wife	18	1
1 male slave	7-14		1
1 male slave	14-30		1

[s.2-237 /142]

Dᵃ TERESA THOMAS	70	1
3 male slaves	14-30		3
1 female slave	14-30		1
living with her:		
Dᵃ MARGARITA LASEBURY	14	1
Dᵃ MARIA ELIZABETH SOBAUCH	45	1
2 sons	7-14	
1 son	14-30	3
2 daughters	7-14	2
1 male slave	14-30		1
1 female slave	14-30	
1 female slave	30-60		2
Dᵃ MARIA ANTONIA RIO	33	1
1 son	14-30	1
4 daughters	14-30	4
living with them:		
MARGARITA MANNEY	33	1
1 daughter	7-14	1
Dⁿ SIMON LUNA	65	1

1814: Outside St. Augustine

Dᴬ MARIA GOLDIN	27	1
1 female slave	14-30		1
D⁽ᴬ⁾ ELIZABETH BROKENSON	22	1
D⁽ᴬ⁾ MARIA GERTRUDIS DEL VALLE	28	1
6 daughters	7-14	6
1 male slave	14-18		1
D⁽ᴬ⁾ ELIZABETH FLORA [HORA?]	70	1
living with her:		
D⁽ᴬ⁾ CLARA FLORA [HORA?]	40	1
1 daughter	14-30	1
D⁽ᴺ⁾ DIEGO SEGUY	74	1
2 sons	14-30	2
D⁽ᴺ⁾ BERNARDO WICKES	26	1
Dᴬ MARIA KUNAN, wife	22	1
D⁽ᴺ⁾ JOSIAH GRAY	32	1
MARIA DOLORES BARNABY, wife	21	1
1 male slave	14-30		1

[s.2–238 /143]

D⁽ᴺ⁾ ENRIQUE GROVE	37	1
D⁽ᴬ⁾ ANA HAMMAN, wife	27	1
1 daughter	7-14	1
living with them:		
D⁽ᴬ⁾ CATALINA HAMMAN	24	1
D⁽ᴬ⁾ CRISTIANA MATARAN	53	1
3 sons	14-30	3
1 daughter	7-14	1
1 daughter	14-30	1
D⁽ᴬ⁾ MARIA GRUBARDY	41	1
1 son	14-30	1
3 daughters	14-30	3
1 male slave	30-60		1
living with them:		
D⁽ᴺ⁾ JUANA MANYAPANY	11	1

1814: Outside St. Augustine

Dᴬ ELIZABETH JURDINE	40	1	
2 sons	14-30	2	
D⁽ᴺ⁾ JORJE CLA	41	1	
Dᴬ ANGELA MESTRE, wife	31	1	
4 daughters	7-14	4	
D⁽ᴺ⁾ GUILLERMO GARBIN	38	1	
1 female slave	30-60		1
D⁽ᴺ⁾ TOMAS STORMES	28	1	
living with him:			
Dᴺ JUAN HERNANDEZ	17	1	
Dᴺ JUAN SHARP	28	1	
MARY VINCENT, wife	28	1	
1 male slave	14-30		1
ELIZA VINCENT	17	1	
Dᴺ FELIPE DEWY	28	1	
Dᴬ MARIA SANCHEZ, wife	19	1	
living with them:			
Dᴬ MARIA SANCHEZ	11	1	
Dᴬ JOSEFA SANCHEZ	8	1	
Dᴬ FRANCISCA	7	1	
8 male slaves	14-30		
5 male slaves	30-60		13
5 female slaves	14-30		5
Dᴺ CARLOS LETON	37	1	
Dᴬ MATILDE SIBBALD	20	1	
			[s.1–239/ 144]
5 male slaves	7-14		5
2 male slaves	14-30		2
Dᴬ GUILLERMO HOBHERK	50	1	
SARAH FENDINE, wife	50	1	
1 son	30-60	1	
2 daughters	30-60	2	
3 male slaves	14-30		3
2 female slaves	14-30		2

1814: Outside St. Augustine

D[N] JUAN RUSSELL	60	1
living with him:		
MARRINA MCINTOSHE	33	1
1 daughter	0-14	1
MAN[L] MACHAD	48	1
living with him:		
ANTONIO TABARES	26	1
LUIS HERNANDEZ	—	1
MARIA VENTURA DELGAD	45	1
living with her:		
FRAN[CA] DE ACOSTA	15	1
1 son	7-14	1
D[N] ANTONIO DE CALA	24	1
living with him:		
D[N] VINCENTE LLARENA	44	1
D[N] JOSE ARREDOND	28	1
living with him:		
D[N] SAMUEL BETTS	30	1
FRANCISCO PEREZ	68	1
MARIA BEATRIS SANCHEZ, wife	30	1
1 son	7-14	
1 son	14-30	2
1 daughter	7-14	1
living with them:		
JUAN CARHANAN	30	1
ENRIQUE KIBLE	54	1
REGINA VEN FIBON, wife	56	1
2 daughters	14-30	2
D[N] GASPAR ROSY	32	1
MATILDA FLORA, wife	34	1
1 son	7-14	1
		[s.1–239 /145]
living with them:		
D[NA] MARIANA DULCET	15	1
D[NA] FRANCISCA SANCHEZ	7	1

1814: Outside St. Augustine

D[N] CARLOS CLARKE	39	1	
living with him:			
PATTY WIGGINS	32	1	
3 sons	7-14	3	
2 daughters	7-14		
1 daughter	14-30	3	
1 male slave	14-30		1
1 female slave	14-30		
1 female slave	30-60		2
D[N] FRANCISCO FATIO	53	1	
D[A] MARIA FATIO	31	1	
1 son	7-14	1	
1 daughter	7-14		
2 daughters	14-30	3	
5 male slaves	7-14		
3 male slaves	14-30		
5 male slaves	30-60		13
4 female slaves	7-14		
6 female slaves	14-30		
5 female slaves	30-60		15
ROBERTO BATLEY	40	1	
D[N] JUAN CARRERAS	22	1	
D[A] MARIA CINTAS	19	1	
D[N] ANTONIO PONS	19	1	
D[N] BARTOLOMEO PONS	19	1	
D[N] JOSE POMAS	18	1	
D[N] JUAN TRIAY	21	1	
D[A] JUANA TRIAY	19	1	
D[N] LORENZO LEONARDO	24	1	
BENJAMIN AYARS	41	1	
1 male slave	14-30		1
SEYMOND PIKET	40	1	
MARIA REBECA, wife	24	1	
1 female slave	14-30		1
MARGARITA MARS	47	1	
1 son	7-14	1	
1 daughter	7-14	1	
1 female slave	30-60		1

_____ 1814: Outside St. Augustine

JUAN RUSKEN	40	1	
ELIZABETH JURDINE	25	1	
1 male slave	30-60		1
D[A] CATALINA CHERKIN	50	1	
2 daughters	14-30	2	
3 male slaves	14-30		3
4 female slaves	14-30		4
D[N] FARGUHAR BETHUNE	32	1	
REBECA SIBBALD, wife	23	1	
2 male slaves	14-30		
2 male slaves	30-60		4
3 female slaves	14-30		3
living with them:			
D[N] CARLOS SIBBALD	23	1	
D[N] SANTIAGO CASHEN	50	1	
D[A] SUSAN KERR	35	1	
5 male slaves	14-30		5
4 female slaves	14-30		4
D[N] ENRIQUE YONGE	44	1	
1 son	14-30	1	
4 male slaves	7-14		
1 male slaves	14-30		5
1 female slave	14-30		1
D[N] DOMINGO ACOSTA	24	1	
living with him:			
D[A] BARBARA ACOSTA	14	1	
D[N] JUAN ACOSTA	8	1	
D[A] JUANA UBERTY	27	1	
1 daughter	7-14	1	

1814: Outside St. Augustine

Part 10: Free People of Color – Light and Dark Skinned

Name	Age	Free	Slave
MARIANA PULE	60	1	
1 son	7-14		
1 son	14-30	2	
living with them:			
VINCENTE DE LA CRUZ	20	1	
MARGARITA VELL	18	1	
JORJE BOUS	34	1	
MARIA CARLOS, wife	34	1	
2 sons	7-14	2	
TORRY TRAVERS	45	1	
CLAY HECTOR, wife	20	1	
FELIX CO—AT[?]	42	1	
living with him			
NANCY PRAMAS	20	1	
MARIA RITE	18	1	
JUAN PETARSON	34	1	
MARIA LIVELY	25	1	
JINA OZANA[?]	32	1	
JUAN MUSE	50	1	
MARIA LUNA, wife	39	1	
DOMINGO SANCO	50	1	
GRES SANCO	22	1	
LUCIA VOLANTIN	22	1	
1 daughter	7-14	1	

1814: Outside St. Augustine

HARRY M^cQUEEN	36	1
DAYNA DOMINGO, wife	38	1
MARIA REYES	21	1
living with them:		
JAYME RIOS	25	1
ANA MARIA	24	1
ISABEL RIVAS	46	1
NANCY RIVAS	19	1
NICOLASA EMBARA	21	1
JOSE SANCHEZ	40	1
— SANCHEZ, wife	35	1
1 male slave	14-30	
1 female slave	7-14	
1 female slave	14-30	2
JUANA WIGGENS	25	1
living with her:		
WILLIAM LILY	8	1
JUANA LILY	9	1

Fernandina
June 8, 1814

Appendix 1:
Table of Abbreviations

ABBREVIATED	NON-ABBREVIATED
Ant°	Antonio
Antª	Antonia
Bart^me	Bartolome
Bautª, B^t	Bautista
Bern^do	Bernardo
Bridª	Brigida
Com^te	Count
Concep^on	Concepcion
D^n	Don (title)
Dª	Doña (title)
Enriq^e	Enrique
Ferd°	Fernando
Fran^ca	Francisca
Fran^c	Francisco
Gab^l	Gabriel
Gov^n	Governor
Hernand^z	Hernandez
Mª	Maria
M^r	Mister
Ig^co	Ignacio
Mag^la	Magdalena
Man^l	Manuel
Manª	Manuela
Marg^ta	Margarita
Mend^z	Mendez
Mig^l	Miguel
Ph^e	Phelipe
Rodrig^z	Ridriguez
Robt°	Roberto
S^r, S^or	Senor (title)
Sª, S^ra	Señora (title)
Urª	Ursula
Vinz^t	Vincent
Xav^r	Xavier

Appendix 2:
Table of Name Conversions

SPANISH	ENGLISH	SPANISH	ENGLISH
Adefonso	Alphonse	Francisco	Francis, Frank
Agata, Agueda	Agatha	Gerardo	Gerald
Almiro	Elmer [?]	Geremias	Jeremiah
Ambrosio	Ambrose	Geronimo	Jerome
Andres	Andrew	Getrudis[z]	Gertrude
Ana	Ann	Gracia	Grace
Anah	Hannah	Gregorio	Gregory
Antonio	Anthony	Gualtero	Walter
Bartolomeo	Bartholomew	Guillermo	William
Bautista	Baptist	Henrique	Henry, Harry
Benedita	Bernadet, Bernice	Ipolito	Hypolite
		Ignacio	Ignace
Benito	Benedict	Ignes	Inez, Agnes
Brigida	Bridget	Isabel, Isabela, Isavel	Elizabeth
Carlos	Charles	Jacobo	Jacob
Carlota	Charlotte	Jaime, Jaimio	James, Jim
Catalina, Catarina	Catherine	Joaquin	Joachim
Cristiana	Christine	Jorje	George
Cristoval	Christopher	José, Josef	Joseph
Dayna	Dinah	Josefa	Josephine
Deophus	Adolphus	Juan	John
Diego	James	Juana	Jane, Jean, Joan
Dionisia, Donisia	Denise	Lucia	Lucinda, Lucy
Dionisio	Dennis	Lorenzo	Lawrence
Domingo	Dominick	Luis, Luiz	Lewis, Louis
Dorotea	Dorothy	Luisa	Louise, Eliza
Eduardo	Edward	Magdalena	Madeleine
Elena	Helen	Marcos	Mark
Enrique	Henry, Harry	Maria	Mary
Esperanza	Hope	Marta, Martina	Martha
Esteban, Esteven	Steven	Matheo, Matias	Matthew
Feby	Phoebe	Michaela	Michelle
Federico	Frederick	Miquel	Michael
Felipe	Phillip	Nicolasa	Nicolette
Fernando	Ferdinand	Pablo	Paul
Francisca	Frances	Pasqual	Pascal

Appendix 2:
Table of Name Conversions
(Continued)

SPANISH	ENGLISH	SPANISH	ENGLISH
Patricio	Patrick	Roefulfo	Ralph [?]
Pedro	Peter	Roque	Roger
Phelipe	Phillip	Santiago	[St.] James
Ramon	Raymond	Sevastian	Sebastian
Ricardo	Richard	Sofia	Sophie
Richeld	Rachel	Teophilo, Tophilo	Theophile
Rodefulfo	Rudolph, Randolph	Thimoteo	Timothy
		Vizente	Vincent

Appendix 3:
Table of Untranslated Terms

SPANISH TERM	DEFINITION
Hacienda	Variously, a country estate, a ranch, or a large area of land.
Lecho	Variously, a river bed, a large row, or a prominent foundation.
Moreno/ morena	A dark-skinned person (male/female) of mixed race.
Mulato/mulata	A mixed-race person (male/female), usually applied by the Spanish to those who are half-white and half-black.
Pardo/parda	A light-brown person (male/female) of mixed race.

Index

Notes

Index

A

Acosta [de Acosta, Costa]
  Barbara 149
  Brigidia Gomez 73
  Catalina 104
  Catalina/Catarina (wife of A. Cantar) 12, 78
  Cicilia Artiles 32, 104
  Domingo 78, 91, 100, 149
  Francisca 147
  Francisca (wife of D. Sanchez) 83
  Francisca Padron 73
  Jorje 20
  Josef 90, 104
  Josefa 104
  Josepha Maria 32
  Juan 73, 81, 150
  Juana (wife of J. Lina) 98
  Lucia 32
  Luis 104
  Margarita Villalonga 90
  Maria 104
  Maria (wife of J. Bulchany) 19, 100
  Maria (wife of N. Mabriti) 78
  Maria Ambros 78
  Maria Braus/Bross 20, 90, 100
  Maria del Carmen 32
  Maria Dremariche 91
  Maria Parla 91
  Maria Rodriguez 104
  Miguel 20, 91
  Pedro 32, 104
  Thomosa 104
Addison, Juan 123, 125
Adeur, Margarita (wife of S. Ashton) 101
Agles, Joseph 12
  Maria Fons 12

Agornes, Ana (wife of J. Arnau) 23
Aguilad, Aguilan [see Aguilar]
Aguilar [Aguilad, Aguilan]
  Catalina 33
  Catalina (wife of A. Guertas) 103, 111
  Catarina 28
  Francisca (wife of J. Rodriguez) 86
  Juan 33, 86, 103
  Melchora Ramos 33, 86, 103
  Tomas 33
Aguirre, Francisco 88
  Maria Sasgarse 67
  Phelipe 88
Akins [see Hyquins]
Albares [see Alvarez]
Alberti [Alberty, Albarty, Albertiny]
  Antonio 100
  Antonio Josef 10, 95
  Catalina/Catarina Oliberas 10, 95
  Christobal 10, 95
  Francisca 10, 95
  Josef 95
  Juan 10, 95
  Juana Maria 22, 95, 101
  Juana Maria (wife of J. Reyes) 10, 22, 82
  Juana Maria Fabregas 95
  Maria 10
  Maria (wife of P. Triay) 100
  Mariana (wife of B. Lopez) 10
  Ursula (wife of C. Llufrio) 88
Albertiny [see Alberti]
Alberty [see Alberti]
Alcina, Antonia 11
  Antonio 11, 97
  Bartolomeo 26, 97
  Benedita 19

Index

Alcina (cont'd)
  Benita (wife of A. Ponz) 97
  Benita Pallicer 97
  Catalina (wife of M. Meina) 95
  Catarina 11
  Juan 10
  Juana (wife of B. Segui) 84
  Margarita 71, 97
  Margarita (wife of A. Reu) 71
  Maria 26, 97
  Maria Luke/Lucas 97
  Miguel 11
  Rafaela 11
  Rafaela Capo 11
Alez, Antonia (wife of A. Roquer) 75
Allon, Juana (wife of J. Welon) 92
Almanas, Manuel 35
  [see also Almara]
Almara, Antonio 87
  Maria Miranda 87
Alvarez [Albarez], Antonia Venz 69
  Antonio Josef 69
  Geronimo 9, 39, 69
  José 143
  Juana (wife of L. Llanez) 76
  Juana Barbe 143
  Mariano 87
  Miguel 69
  Teresa Maria Antonia 69
  Theresa 69
Amadona, Beatrix (wife of M. Chapuz) 71
Ambros [see Bross], Maria (wife of D. Costa) 78
Andrade, Ana Ursula (wife of J. Nixon) 88
  Henrique 88
  Josefa Camena 88
Andrea (slave) 79
Andres [Andrea, Andreu, Anoreu],
  Agueda Pons 11, 98
  Ana 109

Andres (cont'd)
  Ana Jemison 109
  Angela 107
  Angela Caulas 93, 98, 107, 109
  Antonia 19, 78
  Antonio 11, 27, 50, 95, 98, 110, 143
  Catalina 110
  Catarina Pons 27, 29, 109
  Francisca 27, 107, 110, 142
  Jaime 107
  Juan 11, 27, 47, 93, 98, 107, 109, 115
  Juana (wife of J. Carreres) 20, 93
  Juana (wife of J. Pons) 20, 25, 93, 95
  Juana (wife of D. Valls) 93
  Magdalena 11, 98
  Marcos 19, 40, 78
  Margarita 107
  Margarita (wife of G. Hernandez) 143
  Margarita Pretos 27, 107
  Maria 109
  Maria (wife of P. Maestre) 26, 109
  Maria Fuesliny 19
  Maria Mabrumaty 115
  Maria Olibera 95
  Mariana Indori 78
  Miguel 27, 110
  Rafael 19, 78
  Roberto 35, 109
  Thomas 47, 107
  Tomas 27
Anoreu [see Andreu]
Antonio (slave) 71, 79, 93
Aquilliam, Tomas 86
Arango, Maria Josefa (wife of J. de Quesada) 88
Arbisola, Mariana (wife of F. Berta) 73
Aredondo [see Arredondo]
Argulles, Jose 113
  Luisa Catalina 113
Arnau [Hernau], Ana Agornes 23

Index

Arnau (cont'd)
  Antonia 21
  Antonia Ponells 94
  Bernado 10, 26, 44, 107
  Clara 94
  Clara Preta[s] 21, 94
  Diego 97
  Dominga 94
  Francisca 21, 94
  Francisco 21, 41, 94
  Inez Girez 96
  Isabel 86
  Isabel (wife of S. Rugera) 69
  Isabel Bercado 86
  Isabel Ferrer 113
  Isabel Mula 13, 86
  Isabela 13
  Jayme 144
  José 142
  Josef 50, 96
  Joseph 23
  Juan 86, 113
  Juan Francisco 13, 51, 86
  Juana (wife of B. Figuera) 97
  Juana Vicarias 97
  Lieutenant 60
  Magdalena Maunusi 96
  Margarita (wife of J. Roquer) 70
  Maria Mula 107
  Margarita Pasqual 144
  Maria Sans 26, 107
  Martin 107
  Pedro 144
  Santiago 21, 94
Arnez, Dominga (wife of J. Batalini) 73
Arons, Jorje 62
Arredondo [Aredondo, Aredond]
  Antonia Perdomo 94
  Brigidia Gomez 112
  Delanza 94

Arredondo (cont'd)
  Dominga 73
  Dorotea 94
  Fernando 94, 112
  Fernando de la Maza 116
  José 147
  Josef 94
  Josef Maria 94
  Mariana Entralgo 116
  Teresa 94
Artiga, Benito 81
  Elena 81
  Geronima Escalona 81
  Lucia Mendez 81
Artiles, Cecilia (wife of P. Acosta) 104
  Josefa Sardina 104
  Juan 104
Ashton [Asthon, Aston],
  Dorotea Higginbothra 77
  Esabela 129
  Eduardo 5, 57, 77, 101
  Felipe 5
  Guillermo 101
  Juana 101
  Juliana 5
  Margarita Adeur 101
  Maria 101
  Maria (wife of J. Fontanel) 77
  Maria Hinsman 5, 101
  Phelipe 101
  Samuel 5, 101
Assuncion, Agustin 72
  Maria Garcia 72
  Maria Ignacia (wife of J. de Ortegas) 72
Ashton [see Asthon]
Atkinson, Juana (wife of J. Garrtet) 144
  Maria (wife of J. Yonge) 141
Auas, Catalina (wife of M. Papi) 85
Ausima [Ausina], Antonio 47
  Bartholomeo 49

Index

Avero [see Havero]
Ayars, Benjamin   148

B

Bacheri, Angelino   15
   Bartolome   15
   Catarina   15
   Josefa Castell   15
   Pedro   15
Bachos [Backhayse, Beckhonre?],
   Jorje   6, 56
Bailie, Juan   62
Balentine, Guillermo   61
Ball, Elias   52
Balumn, Juan   13
Bannuche, Margarita (wife of A. Luke)   97
Baquery, Angelo   55
Barbara (slave)   94
Barbe, Francisco   143
   Juana (wife of J. Alvarez)   143
Barber, Francisca Garcia   74
   Francisco   74
   Juan   19, 74
   Maria Rosa Segui   74
Barcelo, Juana (wife of B. Slop)   92
   Maria (wife of F. Blasi)   75
Bardoron, Vizente   12
Bargas [see de Bargas]
Barneby [Barnaby], Ana   106
   Ana Gold   106
   Juan   106
   Maria   106
   Maria Dolores (wife of J. Gray)   145
   Santiago   106
   Susanah   106
   Susanah Diegos   106
Barnett, Ana (wife of F. Roche)   89
   Isabel Jomon   89
   Margarita (wife of F. Roch)   32
   Thomas   89
Barrios, Andres   38
Barter, Gaspar   64

Batalini [Bateliny], Dominga Arnez   73
   Josef   52, 73
   Joseph   14
   Juan Bautista   73
Bateliny [see Batalini]
Batley, Roberto   148
Batuarte, Catalina (wife of M. Rengil)
   103
   Eulalia Olives   13
   Francisco   13
Bausa [see Bousa]
Bautista, Juan   13, 55, 65
Baya, Antonio   92
   Josef   92
   Joseph   20
   Juana Ximenez   20, 92
Bearding, Guillermo   129
   Juan   129
Beatris (free mulatto)   35
Becardo, Isabel (wife of J. Arnau)   86
Beckhonre [see Bachos]
Belisle, Alexandro   79
   Ana (wife of M. Gutreau)   79
   Maria Blanca   79
Belory [see Velroy]
Beltido, Antonia Fornalis   85
   Catalina   85
   Clara   85
   Francisco   85
   Josef   85
   Josefa Moreno   85
Bendicho, Francisca   80
   Francisco   80
   Manuel Fernandez   80
   Maria Rodriguez   80
Bergallo, José   143
Bernal, Catalina (wife of R. Torres)   72
Berrio [Berrios, Barrios],
   Andres   38
   Maria Antonia de Palma   73
   Pedro Diaz   73

---------- Index

Berrio (cont'd)
   Salvador 73
Berta, Antonio 18, 37, 46, 73
   Francisco 73
   Lorenzo 73
   Maria Sanz/Zans 18, 73
   Mariana 73
   Mariana Arbisola 73
Bethune, Farquhar 149
   Rebeca Sibbald 149
Betts, Samuel 147
Billa [see Villa]
Bilot, Abigail 70
   Georje 70
   Juan 70
   Juan, Jr. 70
   Miguel 70
   Rebecca Crandel 69
Blanca [Blanco], Josef 71
   Maria (wife of A. Belisle) 79
   Maria Antonia Mans 71
   Maria Josefa (wife of J. Busquet) 71
   Josef 71
   Juana 71
Blas [Blasi], Francisco 32, 75
   Juan 75, 87
   Juan Miguel 32
   Margarita Redondo 32
   Maria Barcelo 75
Blent, Richeld (wife of R. Mory) 4
Blos (slave) 94
Bobinson [Robinson], Barbara (wife of J. Kevy) 84
   Margarita Davison 84
   Miguel 84
Bodlam, Juan Glodo 12
Bogin, Guillermo 62
Bohan, Margarita (wife of P. la Febre) 79
Bonely, Josef 55, 67
Bousa [Bous, Bausa], Eulalia Olivas 13
   Francisca 41

Bousa (cont'd)
   Francisco 13
   Jorje 150
   Maria Carlos 150
Bousquet [see Busquet]
Bovier, Ana (wife of V. Fitzpatrick) 72
   Maria 72
   Ricardo 72
Bowden, Isack, Sr. 66
   Issack 66
   Moses 129
Bowin, Ana (wife of G. Welsh) 86
Boyce, Isavel 57
Boyke, Agustin 110
   Maria Catalina 110
   Pedro 110
Bracien, Catalina Norwart 86
   Guillermo 86
   Isabel (wife of A. Leslie) 86
Brabo [see Brava] 116
Braddock, Guillermo 133
   Juan 133
Brass [Braus, Bross],
   Catalina (wife of J. Parla) 91
   Maria (wife of D. Acosta/Costa) 90, 100
   Maria (wife of D. Tudidache) 20
   [see also Ambros]
Braus [see Brass]
Brava [Bravo, Brabo], Cristobal 115
   Josefa Legas 115
   Maria de los Agelos Prado 83
   Maria Rita (wife of J. Sanchez) 29, 83
   Thomas 83
Brazo, Domingo Escergopory del 11
Brewer, Carlos 139
   Francisco 139
Briton, Sarah (wife of J. Scot) 86
Brokenson, Elizabeth 145

Index

Bross [see Brass]
Brown [Bron], Andres 24, 98
   Catalina (wife of J. Garcia) 70
   Inez Purla 98
   Pedro 72
Buchantini [Buchantiny, Buchentini]
   Catalina Coll 14, 74
   Luis 14, 53, 74
   Miguel 74
   Rosa Piumbi 74
Buchany [Bulchany, Buchoni]
   Felicia Marialy 100
   Guillermo 100
   Josef 40, 100
   Joseph 19
   Juan 143
   Maria Costa/Acosta 19, 100
   Miguel 100
   Nicolas 100
   Rosa Maria 100
Buchentiny [see Buchantiny]
Bunch, C. 125
   Juan 123, 125
Burden, Isach, Jr. 65
Burgo [see Peso de Burgo]
Busquet [Bousquet], Augustina Maria 71
   Josef 71
   Josef Gabriel 71
   Josef Maria 71
   Josefa Blanca 116
   Juan 116
   Juan Josef 71
   Juan Ricardo 32
   Maria Blanco 71
   Sebastiana de Fuentes 71
Bustan, Ricardo 29

C

Caballero, Juana (wife of M. Quintana) 97
Cabedo [see Cavedo]
Camena, Josefa (wife of H. Andrade) 88
Camp, Juana 81
Campan, Juana (wife of B. Toro) 81
Campino, Magdalena (wife of N. Segui) 100
Campos
   Antonia (wife of J. Triay) 78
   Esperansa (wife of D. Ramillera) 93
   Margarita (wife of P. Carreras) 93
   Margarita (wife of P. Tremol) 93
   Maria (wife of F. Pratts) 91
Camugina, Geronima (wife of P. Peso de Burgo) 78
Candelaria, Jose 144
   Juana Segui 144
Cane, Agueda Seguera 87
   Bartolome 87
   Margarita (wife of L. Capo) 87
Canela, Maria (wife of G. Gonsopli) 94
Canobas [Canovas], Antonio 13, 51, 85
   Bartolomeo 85
   Catarina Maestre 13, 85
   Juana Redevetes 85
   Martin 85
Cantal, Catalina (wife of J. Nifuelas) 87
Cantar [Canter], Agustin 12, 78
   Antonio 12, 45, 78
   Catarina Acosta/Costa 12, 78
   Domingo 12, 78
   Maria 12, 78
   Patricio 12, 78
   Praides Venent 78
Canto, Carlos 141, 142
   Luisa (wife of S. Argulles) 113
Capela [Capella, Capele] Ana 21, 70
   Ana Veri 70
   Andres 50
   Catalina Duran 109
   Francisco 21, 70
   Geronima 24, 109
   Jeronima Suau 109

Index

Capela (cont'd)
  José 70
  Lorenzo 24, 45, 109
  Luis 70
  Margarita 54
  Margarita Guibarnau 21
  Margarita Roquer 70
  Maria (wife of J. Ponz) 78
  Mateo 109
  Mathias 109
Capman, Guillermo 64
Capo [Capot]
  Agueda Segui [Seguera] 26, 109
  Antonia Mesguilson 109
  Antonio 16, 87, 95
  Catalina 99
  Esparania Mall 109
  Gabriel 26, 109
  Getrudis Pacety 142
  Juan 16, 26, 53, 109
  Lorenzo 16, 42, 87
  Margarita Cane 87
  Maria Cintas 109
  Maria de los Dolores 87
  Miguel 95
  Pedro 23, 26, 109, 141
  Rafaela 16, 87
  Rafaela (wife of A. Alcina) 11
  Rafaela (wife of A. Meina) 95
  Rafaela Fabregas 87, 95
Cardona, Lorenzo 90
  Magdalena (wife of J. Hernandez) 98
  Margarita 75, 95, 97
  Margarita (wife of A. Ponz) 95
  Margarita (wife of J. Sambias) 75
  Margarita Mila 90
  Maria Ana (wife of J. Villa) 18
  Mariana (wife of J. Villalonga) 90
Carelli, Agueda 15
  Catarina Venz 15
  Getrudis 28

Carelli (cont'd)
  Pedro 15
  Vizente 15
Careras [Carreras, Carreres]
  Clara Pasceti 89
  Diego 20, 47, 89
  Getrudis 89
  Getrudis (wife of P. Pons) 141
  Josef 47, 93
  Joseph 20
  Juan 20, 22, 52, 82, 89
  Juana 93, 148
  Juana Andrea 20, 93
  Margarita 22, 82
  Margarita Campos 93
  Margarita Perpal 82
  Maria 20, 82, 89, 93
  Maria Triay 22, 82, 89
  Pedro 93
Carhanan, Juan 147
Carillo [Carilo, Carila], Ana 83
  Francisca Rodriguez 71, 83
  Francisco 71, 83
  Getrudiz (wife of M. Chapus) 28, 71
Carlos, Maria (wife of J. Bous) 150
Carrel, Ana (wife of J. Travers) 83
Carter, Hepuorth 106
  Isabel 106
  Margarita Maria 106
  Margarita MacLean 106
  Maria 106
  Maria Hepourth 106
  Thomas 106
  Thomas Manuel 106
Casada, Esteban 77
  Juan 77
Casalo, Tecla (wife of A. Marin) 71
Casaly [Casaty], Agueda 85
  Agueda (wife of B. Suarez) 85
  Antonio 85
  Catalina Redivetes 79, 85
  Pedro 79

Index

Casaly (cont'd)
  Vicente 45, 79, 85
Casanovas, Antonia (wife of R. Indori) 78
Casaty [see Casaly]
Cashen, Santiago 149
Casilda [Casitoa], Isabel Vicenta 79, 86
Casilda y Puima [see Puima]
Castaneda [see Castenada]
Cassella, Josefa 55
Castel [Castell]
  Agueda Segui 82, 89
  Antonia 96
  Antonia (wife of P. Riso) 96
  Bartolome 82, 89
  Josefa (wife of A. Bacheri) 15
  Juana (wife of D. Seguy) 11, 74, 82
  Margarita 26
  Maria (wife of A. Paceti) 17, 89
  Maria (wife of J. Segui) 17, 89
Castenada [Castaneda], Gaspar 91
  Maria 91
  Maria (wife of J. Ortegas) 92
  Maria (wife of J. Sanchez) 91
  Sebastiana de Bargas 91
Castillo, Catalina Hota 114
  Ramon 114
Castro y Ferrer, Antonia 112
  Bartolome 112
Catalina (slave) 81
Catrinaricha, Catalina (wife of T. Hedsorcopli) 82, 100
Caulas, Angela 93
  Angela (wife of J. Andreu) 93, 98, 107, 109
  Antonio 93
  Juana Ponz 93
Cavedo [Cabedo, Cavio] [see also Quevedo]
  Ana Maria (wife of S. Hortegas) 90

Cavedo (cont'd)
  Inez 77, 90
  Inez (wife of P. Coufacio) 17, 77
  Inez (wife of A. Gererino) 77
  Inez Vestorin 90
  Inez Victoria/Victurina 74, 77, 90
  Juan 42, 90
  Juana Segui 90
  Mariana (wife of D. Martinely) 74
  Santiago 74, 77, 90
Cayetano 35
Cerona, Geronima (wife of P. Solana) 76
Cescaloma, Antonia Quinomez 84
  Diego 84
  Manuel 84
Ceveris, Maria (wife of J. de Salas) 83
Chacon, Manuela Belen (wife of D. Reyes) 80
Chanapoly, Juan 43, 54
Chapus [Chapuz], Beatrix Amadona 71
  Getrudiz Carrillo 28, 31,
  Josef 71
  Josef Jillan 28, 71
  Miguel 28, 35, 71
Chato, Agueda Coll 14
  Juan 14
Chaunico, Juan 48
Chenovant, Juan 41
Cherez, Ana (wife of S. Hortegas) 99
  Lorenzo 99
  Maria Hernandez 99
Cherkin, Catalina 149
Christie, Elijah 128
Christopher, Guillermo 134
  Lewis 132
  Spicer 60, 134
Cintas, Antonia Reu 71
  Bartolomeo 51, 71
  Bineto 71
  Josefa (wife of B. Coll) 74
  Juana (wife of J. Espineta) 94, 105

Index

Cintas (cont'd)
  Juana (wife of A. Pallicer) 105
  Juana Juvera 71
  Magdalena 71
  Maria 109, 148
  Maria (wife of J. Capo) 109
Cla, Angela Maestre 146
  Antonia 98
  Georje 98
  Inez Purla 98
  Jorje 24, 46, 98, 146
  Josef 46
  Maria Pritos 98
Clak, Andres Bron 24
  Antonia 24
  Inez Pablo 24
  Jorje 24
Clapton, Sarah (wife of J. Powel) 80
Clark [Clarke], Angus 66
  Carlos 148
  Diege 56, 92
  Georje 144
  Gualtero Carlos 81
  Gualtero Witter 5
  Honoria 4, 34, 40, 48, 57, 67, 68, 79, 81, 92, 131, 137, 138
  Jorje 4
  Josef 58, 79
  Margarita 4, 81, 92
  Margarita Czerich 6
  Santiago 6, 81
  Thomas 79, 81
Claveria, Thimoteo Howard y 5
Clavero, Rosa (wife of M. Ximenes) 84
Clotworthy, Diego 65
Cobachichosa, Josef 55
Coll, Agueda (wife of R. Leonardi) 14, 103
  Bartolomeo 74, 100, 103
  Catalina (wife of L. Buchantini) 14, 74
  Francisca (wife of M. Ponz) 85, 109

Coll (cont'd)
  Francisca Ponz 99
  Josef 100
  Josefa (wife of J. Femenias) 76
  Josefa Cintas 74
  Josepha (wife of N. Nicolic) 19, 100
  Josepha Ponz 19, 100
  Lorenzo 13, 39
  Margarita Villa 17, 99
  Pedro 17, 99
  Sebastian 17, 41, 99
Collin [Collen, Collens, Collins]
  Ana 5
  Cecilia Juliana 69
  Juliana 13
  Juan Bautista 13, 69, 115
  Maria 5
  Maria Rosa Ana 69
Colston, Thomas 65
Contreras, Luis 29
Coonon [see Kunan]
Cordero [Cordery], Estevan 6
  Leonor Gonzales 29
  Maria Leaswell 6, 29
  Thomas 6, 29, 35, 58
  Thomas Francisco 35
Cortes, Agueda Segui 102
  Antonio 102
  Claudio 102
  Dimas 102
  Josef 91
  Sebastiana Quesada 102
Cortinas, Pablo 39
Coruna, Antonio 31, 104
  Francisco 33
  Josef 104
  Josef Antonio 31, 104
  Josefa Garcia 104
  Juana Escalona 33
  Lucia 36
  Lucia (wife of M. Martinez) 104

Index

Coruna (cont'd)
   Lucia Antonia 31
   Manuela Garcia 104
   Manuela Sanchez 31
   Maria Dolores 33
   Pablo 33
   Pedro 104
   Ursula Suarez 104
Cosifacho [see Coufacio]
Costa [see Acosta]
Coufacio [Cosifacho], Inez Cavedo 17, 77
   Jacob 77
   Marta 18, 77
   Marta Notachisa 77
   Pedro 17, 77
   Praredis 18, 77
   Theodoro 77
Cousons, Maria (wife of M. Ogden) 97
Cowen, Roberto 66
Crandel, Rebecca (wife of J. Bilot) 70
Crespel, Maria Magdalena (wife of F. Facio) 4
Crespin (slave) 70
Crissiano 35
Crosby, Maria (wife of F. Morlan) 99
Cross, Juana 4, 56
Cruz [see de la Cruz]
Cuella [Cuello], Antonia 75
   Antonia Perez 75
   Antonia Pons 75
   Antonio 75
   Diego 75
   Maria Manuela 75
   Santiago 38
Cummings, Honoria (wife of T. Clark) 79, 81
   Santiago 81
Czerich, Margarita (wife of S. Clark) 6

D

Dalmedo [see del Medo]
Dalton, Ana (wife of J. McQuien) 88
Daly, Juana (wife of G. Nickleron) 75
Damaso (slave) 70
Danbrooks, Lucia (wife of A. Leslie) 86
Davison, Margarita (wife of M. Bobinson) 84
Dawrino, Ana (wife of G. Smith) 108
   Ana Farrell 108
   Patricio 108
de Acosta [see Acosta]
de Aguilar, Francisca 112
   [see also Aguilar]
de Almanza, Antonia 101
   Felicita Josefa 101
   Francisco 101
   Josefa de Troya y Rugera 101
   Juan Antonio 101
   Luisa Perez 101
   Manuel 101
   Paula 101
de Antiles, Cicilia (wife of P. de Acosta) 32
de Aribas, Maria Gracia Perpal 92
   Maria Isabel 92
   Raymundo 92
   Tudeo 92
   Ursela 92
   Ursela de Avero 92
de Avero, Ursela (wife of R. de Aribas) 92
de Bargas, Sebastina (wife of G. Castenada) 91
   Sebastina (wife of A. Escalona) 93
de Ben [Deven], Manuel 31, 38, 117
de Burgo [see Peso de Burgo]
de Cala, Ana Maria de los Dolores Segui 95
   Antonio 95, 147
   Juan 95
   Juana 95
   Lucas 95

Index

de Cala (cont'd)
   Manuel Josef 95
   Pedro 31, 37, 95
de Casas, Maria (wife of D. de
   Zubraneta) 86
de Cordoba, Maria 93
de Fuentes [see Fuente], Antonio 77
   Gregoria Silva 77
   Maria Pery 77, 114
   Ramon 77, 114
   Sebastiana (wife of J. Busquet) 71
de Gasino y Lernen, Ana Perren 87
   Bartolomeo 87
   Santiago 87
de Ita y Salacar, Eugenia 91
   Geronimo 84, 91
   Francisca 84, 91
   Juana Havero 84, 91
de la Asencion, Maria 88
de la Crux, Vicente 150
de la Pisente, Ferdinando 116
   Leonor Lowe 116
de la Rosa, Beatriz (wife of B. Pons) 100
   Juana Perez 71
   Juana Sanchez (wife of J. de Salas) 83
de Lasaga, Inez Generino 77
   Joaquin 77
   Maria Rosa Dias 77
   Mariano 77
   Marinda 77
de Leon, Domingo Rodriguez 52
   [see also Leon]
de Lias, Rosa (wife of F. Sanchez) 98
de los Ijuelos, Catalina 42, 116
de los Monturos, Juana Montes (wife
   of C. Gonzales) 102
de Nuncio, Magdalena 94
de Oca [see Montes de Oca]
de Ortegas
   [see also Hortegas, Ortega]

de Ortegas (cont'd)
   Francisca 72
   Francisco 72
   Ignacia Antonia 72
   Josef 72
   Juana Nepomuncia 72
   Maria Dias 72
   Maria Ignacia Assuncion 72
   Maria Josefa 72
de Palma, Antonio 32, 37, 73
   Elvira Quintero 73
   Juan 73
   Juana Elvira 32, 73
   Margarita MacFeal 32, 73
   Maria 73
   Maria Antonia (wife of P. Berrio) 73
de Paula, Francisca 77
de Porras, Catalina (wife of J. Ponze
   de Leon) 93
   Juana Navarra 93
   Salbador 93
de Quesada, Juan N. 88
   Manuela 88
   Maria de la Asencion 88
   Maria Josefa Arango 88
   Rafael 88
   Vicente 88
de Salas, Clemente 83
   Juan 83, 102
   Juan Antonio 83
   Juan Pablo Manuel 102
   Juana Margarita 83
   Juana Sanchez (de la Rosa) 83, 102
   Julian 102
   Maria Ceveris 83
   Teresa de Jesus Rodriguez 102
de San Lorenzo, Margarita (wife of D.
   Jinandy) 72
de Soria, Josef Fernandez 86
   Maria (wife of J. de Zubraneta) 86

Index

de Soria (cont'd)
    Vicente 86
de Soto, Catalina (wife of J. Sanchez) 91
de Tores, Paula 28, 81
    [see also Torres]
de Troya y Reguera, Josefa (wife of F. de Almanza) 100
de Zubraneta, Domingo 86
    Josefa 86
    Lorenzo Juan Manuel 86
    Maria de Casas 86
    Maria de Soria 86
del Brazo, Domingo Escerpory 11
    Geronima Ibarnau 11
del Canto
    [see also Ruis del Canto]
    Francisca de Ita y Salazar 84
    Francisco Ruis 84
    Geronima Escalona 84
    Juan 84
    Luisa 84
del Corral, Felix 77
    Francisca (wife of G. Zamorano) 77
    Juana Diso Menocal 77
del Medo [Dalmedo], Ana Maria 23, 99
    Francisco 22, 99
    Josef 99
    Juan 99
    Juana Manent 22, 99
    Juana Vens 22
    Pedro 23
del Pozo, Magdalena (wife of S. Trual) 94
del Toro, Fernanda Escalona 72
    Juan 72
    Juan Josef 36, 72
    Rafaela Escalona 72
    Rosalia Ponze de Leon 72
    Thomasa Margarita 72
del Valle, Maria Gertrudis 145

Delgado [Delgad], Basilia (wife of J. Acosta) 81
    Juan 81
    Maria Ventura 147
    Petrona Gomez 81
Deven [see de Ben]
Dewy, Felipe 146
    Maria Sanchez 146
Dias [Diaz], Antonio 143
    Josef 74
    Maria (wife of F. de Ortegas) 72
    Maria de los Dolores Miranda 74
    Maria Rosa (wife of J. Lasaga) 77
    Micaela Fuentes 74
    Pedro Berrio 73
    Rafael 74
Diego (free Negro) 8
Diegos, Susana (wife of J. Barneby) 106
Dimalachy, Maria 21
    Nicolas 21
    Pedro 21, 54
Dionisio 68
Dogharty, Juan 63
Dominga, Danya (wife of H. McQueen) 94, 150
Dominguez, Carlos 115
    Maria Muro 115
Douglas, Maria (wife of M. Malter) 108
Dremariche [Drimarch]
    [see also Dimalachy]
    Catalina Femenias 91
    Domingo 91
    Maria (wife of M. Costa) 91
    Pedro 54
Druly, Isabel (wife of J. Purcel) 80
Duff, Ana (wife of A. Leslie) 79
Dulzet [Dulcet], Josef 74
    Maria Scerte 74
    Mariana 147
    Pedro 74

Dupont, Abraham 105
 Ana 105
 Gueido 105
 Isabel Goodbee 105
 Josef 105
 Juana Isabel 105
 Juana Isabel Dupree 105
 Maria Magdalena 105
 Rebecca 105
 Rosina (wife of F. Holzendorf) 106
 Rosina 106
Dupree, Juana Isabel (wife of A. Dupont) 105
Duran [Doran], Catalina (wife of L. Capela) 109
 Groves 6, 57
 Inez Paulo/Purla 109
 Pedro 98, 109
Durante, Pedro 24
Duvignón, Leon 116

E

Eager, Rosa, 62
Eastlake, Samuel 66
Echauarria, Juan Josef 12
Edwards, Juan 139
Ellerbee, Juan 79
 Sarah Mulcartre 79
 Thomas 79
Embara, Felicia Sanchez 116
 Felipe 116
 Nicolasa 151
Englada, Maria (wife of F. Triay) 92
English, Jayme 142
Engrago [see Entargo]
Ennrique [see Henrique]
Ensenada, Margarita (wife of R. Paredes) 82
Entargo [Entrago, Entralgo, Engrago], Catalina Nifuelas 87

Entargo (cont'd)
 Clara 87
 Francisco 87
 Isabel Rodriguez 87
 Juan Antonio 87
 Juan Blos 87
 Manuel 87
 Maria 87
 Maria (wife of F. Arredondo) 116
Entes, Josef 50
Entrago, Entralgo [see Entargo]
Erhardt, Francisco 106
 Isabel (wife of J. Holzendorf) 106
 Maria 106
Escalona, Alonzo 93
 Fernanda 72
 Geromina (wife of B. Artiaga) 81
 Geronima (wife of J. Ruis del Canto) 84
 Joaquin 36, 72
 Josefa 72
 Juana (wife of P. Coruna) 33
 Lucia 30
 Luisa 93
 Phelipa Llanez 72
 Rafaela (wife of J. del Toro) 72
 Sebastiana Bargas 93
 Thomas 72
 Thomosa M. 72
Escobal, Ana Maria (wife of P. Rodriguez) 79
Escudero, Antonio 71
 Juana Mir 71
 Magdalena (wife of F. Marin) 21, 71, 85
Esperania, Maria (wife of J. Venazulace) 87
Espineta [Espinete], Antonia 95
 Antonia (wife of M. Gracias) 26
 Catalina 95
 Catalina (wife of R. Ximenez) 93

Index

Espineta (cont'd)
 Francisca 94
 Francisco 20, 94
 Josef 54, 94
 Joseph 20
 Juan 94
 Juana Cintas 94
 Margarita 95
 Maria Treal 20, 94
Espinosa, Agustina de los Monturos 102
 Antonia (wife of J. Sanchez) 70, 79
 Diego 70
 Josefa 28, 36, 70
 Josefa Torres 70
 Sebastian 28, 70
Estacholi [Estacholy, Stacoly],
 Barbara 13, 76
 Barbara (wife of M. Mabrite) 143
 Barbara Leon 13, 76
 Bartolomeo 13, 76
 Domingo 13, 76, 142
 Francisco 13, 76, 115
 Jorje 51
 Maria Legas 115
 Maria Petros 13, 76
 Ursula Llufrio 142
Estefanopoly [Estevanoply, Estepanopli, Stefanopli], Elias 85
 Francisco 15, 85
 Jorje 4
 Juana 15, 85
 Juana Marin 15, 33, 83, 85
 Malta 15
 Maria (wife of J. Gutierros) 83
 Marta 15, 85
 Nicolas 15, 41, 83, 85
Esteve [Esteves], Catarina 14
 Francisco 14
 Juan 14
 Juana 14
 Juana Salon 14

Esteve (cont'd)
 Sevastian 14
 Simon 42
Esthers, Jesse 68
Estopa [Stopa], Ana Quintana 25, 97
 Margarita 25
 Margarita Pallicer 97
 Pedro 25, 43, 55, 65, 97
Eusa, Pedro 23
Euberty, Antonio 51
Euget, Agueda (wife of F. Ponz) 91
Eundori [see Indori]
Evens, Maria 4

F

Fabregas, Juana Maria (wife of C. Alberti) 95
 Rafaela (wife of A. Capo) 87, 95
Facio [Fatio, Favio], Francisco 64, 73, 148
 Francisco Felipe 4, 56
 Juan 109
 Luis 64
 Maria 148
 Maria Magdalena Crespel 4
 Sophia [Sofia] Maria Phelipina [Felipina] (wife of J. Flemming) 4, 73
 Ursela M. 73
Falany [see Felany]
Farrell, Ana (wife of P. Dawrino) 108
Fatany, Ferdnando 52
Fatio [see Facio]
Faulks, Sarah 129
Faustina, Rosalia (wife of F. Huet) 29
Favio [see Facio]
Felany [Falany], Fernando 9, 105
 Margarita 9, 105
 Margarita Belroy/Velroy 9, 105
 Maria 9
 Santiago 9, 105

Index

Felany (cont'd)
Teresa 9, 105
Femenias, Catalina 105
   Catalina (wife of D. Dremariche) 91
   Jaime 76
   Josefa (wife of P. Garcia) 76
   Josepha 19
   Josepha Coll 19, 76
   Margarita (wife of F. Pellicer) 76
Fendine, Sarah (wife of G. Hobherk) 146
Fernandez, Ana Sanchez 116
   Domingo 137
   Francisca (wife of A. Guiterros) 83
   Jose 116
   Josefa (wife of V. de Soria) 86
   Juan 102, 115
   Ramona Solano 102
   Santiago 102
Fernaris, Antonia (wife of P. Sanz) 11
Ferrer [Ferren], Ana 23
   Ana (wife of S. de Gasino y Lerner) 87
   Ana (wife of P. Venz) 99
   Isabel (wife of J. Arnau) 113
   Josef 105
   Juan 105
   Juana Hocha 105
   Margarita 99
   Maria (wife of J. Segui) 82
   Maria (wife of F. Villa) 95–96, 105
Ferreyna, Antonio 88
   Francisco Lorenzo 88
   Garcia Maria Fonteoa 88
   Isabel Nixon 88
   Juan 88
   Juan Bautista 88
   Maria 88
Fesua [Fezua], Agueda 16
   Francisca Pretos 22
   Juan 16
   Pedro 22
Fiby (free Negro) 70

Figuera [Figueras, Figueray], Bartolomeo 44, 97
   Diego 97
   Juana 97
   Juana Arnau 97
   Juana Pomer 97
   Miguel 44, 97
Fillera, Bartolomeo 11
   Diego 11
   Juana 11
   Juana Hernau 11
   Miguel 11
Finandes, Domingo 72
   Juana Torres 72
   Margarita de San Lorenzo 72
   Miguel 72
   Miguel Lorenzo 72
Fiol, Antonia (wife of P. Villa) 91, 99
Fir, Josef 94
Fis [Fish], Geremias 8
   Jesse 52
Fitzgerald, Geraldo 83
   Isabel Coonon 83
   Lucia 137
   Maria (wife of T. Travers) 83
Fitzpatrick, Ana Bovier 72
   Ana Gillard 72
   Eugenio 72
   Francisco 72
   Guillermo 138
   Pedro Francisco 72
   Valentin 72
Fleming [Flemming], Jorje 4, 73
   Maria Welsh 73
   Sophia [Sofia] Maria Philipina [Felipina] Facio 4, 73
   Thomas 73
Fletcher, Guillermo 124, 126
Flora [Hora], Clara 145
   Elizabeth 145
   Matilda (wife of G. Rosy) 147

Index

Flucha, Juana (wife of J. Ferrer) 105
Flusa, Catalina (wife of J. Gomila) 79
Fod, Lindsey 130
Fonno, Thomas 59
Fons, Francisco 12
    Maria (wife of J. Agles) 12
Fontanel, Antonia Lago 75, 77
    Francisca de Paula 77
    Josef 77, 115
    Maria Aston/Ashton/Houston 77, 115
    Maria Lucia Rodriguez 75
    Pedro 75
Fonteoa, Gracia Maria (wife of A. Ferreyna) 88
Foraster [see Forraster]
Forbes, Juan 130
Ford [see Fod]
Fornalis,
    [see also Furnelles]
    Antonia (wife of J. Beltido) 85
    Clara Ponz 85
    Juan 85
Forraster [Foraster], Brigida MacDonnel 89
    Donisia Hill/Hull 89
    Isabel 89
    Juan 4
    Gerado 89
    Patricio 89
    Susanah 89
    Thomas 89
Francisca (slave) 93
Fraser, Juan 131
Frecy, Juan 131
Frost, Jesse 66
Fuchia [Fuxia], Francisca Pretos 107
    Josef 107
    Margarita Llesano 107
    Pedro 44, 107
Fudichy, Antonio 45
    [see also Tudichy]

Fuente [Fuentes], Micaela (wife of J. Dias) 74
Fuesliny, Mariana (wife of M. Andres) 19
Fuixa [see Fuchia]
Furnelles, Juan 78
    Juana Quintana 78
    Pedro 78
    [see also Fornalis]
Furdas, Josef 55
    [see also Turdas]

G

Galen, Juan 92
    Manuela Inero 92
    Maria Dolores (wife of P. Salzedo) 92
Gamugina, Geronima (wife of P. Peso de Burgo) 78
Garbin, Guillermo 146
Garcia, Catalina Brown 70
    Clemente 76
    Dominga 76
    Francisca (wife of F. Barber) 74
    Josefa (wife of J. Coruna) 104
    Josefa Femenias 76
    Josefa Ortegas 92
    Juan 92, 104
    Juan Antonio 70
    Lucia Sanchez 104
    Magdalena 70
    Manuela (wife of J. Coruna) 104
    Maria Ignacia (wife of A. Assuncion) 72
    Maria Sanchez 92
    Miguel 50
    Pedro 32, 38, 76
    Sebastian 92
Gardner, Guillermo 129
Garrtet, Jose 144

Index

Garrtet (cont'd)
  Juana Atkinson 144
Gavardy, Antonio 100
  Catalina/Catarina Olibera 10, 100
  Maria (wife of J. Turdas) 100
  Maria Magdalena 10, 100
Generino [Ginirini], Antonio 17, 77
  Ines 18
  Inez (wife of M. de Lasaga) 77
  Inez Cabedo 77
  Maria Rosa 18, 77
Genoble [Genoply], Ana 108
  Leonora/Elonora (wife of A. Hinsman) 6, 108
  Juan 108
Gernon, Guillermo 90
  Juan 90
  Maria Hacket 90
  Thomas 90
Geynon, Andres 76
  Gillermo 76
  Margarita 76
  Maria 76
Gilbert, Juan 129
  Roberto 129
Gillard, Ana (wife of E. Fitzpatrik) 72
Girez, Inez (wife of J. Arnau) 96
Gold, Ana (wife of S. Barnaby) 106
Goldin, Maria 145
Gomez, Antonia (wife of A. Lopez) 96
  Antonia Triay 96
  Antonia Tudoni 99
  Bernardo 81
  Blanca Segui 113
  Brigida (wife of F. Arredondo) 112
  Brigida (wife of M. Guadarama) 73
  Eusebio 81, 113
  Francisca (wife of B. Velez) 73
  Inez Mendez 73, 81
  Josef 73, 81
  Josef Maria 81

Gomez (cont'd)
  Josefa 73
  Juan 81
  Juana (wife of L. Trutilon) 99
  Maria 81
  Maria Rodriguez 81, 94
  Martin 96, 99
  Nicolas 81
  Nicolasa 30, 94
  Nicolasa (wife of T. Arredondo) 94
  Pedro 81, 94
  Petrona (wife of J. Delgado) 81
Gomila [Gomilla], Catalina 79
  Catalina Flusa 79
  Dorotea (wife of M. Hernandez) 10, 79
  Joaquin 79
  Josef 52, 79
  Joseph 10
Gonsopoli, Gorje 94
  Juan 94
  Maria Canela 94
Gonzales, Ana Ceres 23
  Antonio 102
  Antonio Joseph 29
  Christostimo 29
  Ipolito 29
  Joaquina (wife of F. Zamorano) 77
  Joseph 29
  Juan 34
  Juan Eugenio 29
  Juan Joseph 29
  Juana de Dios 29
  Juana Montes de Oca 29, 102
  Juana Suarez 81
  Leonarda 102
  Leonarda Josefa 29
  Leonor (wife of T. Cordero) 29
  Luisa 81
  Maria (wife of R. Sahabedra) 102
  Miguel Ipolito 35

Index

Gonzales (cont'd)
   Roque 81
Goodbee, Ana (wife of G. Dupont) 105
Gouson, Margarita (wife of A. MacDonnel) 72
Gracias, Antonia Espineta 26
   Margarita 26
   Maria Perpal 92
   Miguel 26
Gray, Josiah 145
   Juan 65
   Maria Dolores Barnaby 145
Griffin, Daniel 5
Griffiths, Cornelio 63
Grove, Ana Hamman 145
   Enrique 145
Grubardy, Maria 145
Grynaldy, Eulalia Olivas 13
   Peregry 13
   Spirion 13
Guadarama [Guadorroma], Brigidia Gomez 73
   Cirilia (wife of M. Huertas) 113
   Francisca Padron 73
   Juan Antonio 734
   Juana de Acosta 73
   Mateo 73, 74
Guanz, Maria 109
Gudden, Francisco 72
   Juan Hopkins 72
   Maria Hopkins 72
Guertas [Huertas], Agueda Dorotea 103
   Antonio 103
   Arimes 103
   Catalina Aguilar 103
   Cirilia Guadorroma 113
   Juan 113
   Juan Antonio 103
   Luisa Rupir 103

Guet, Francisco 55
   Francisco Josef 35
   [see also Huet]
Guibarnau, Margarita 21
Guillermo (free mulatto) 9
Guiterros, Andres 83
   Francisca Fernandez 83
   Juan 83
   Maria Estefanopoly 83
Guscain, Ricardo 64
Gutreau, Ana Belisle 79
   Maria (wife of P. la Febre) 93
   Martin 79

H

Hacket, Maria (wife of G. Gernon) 90
   Maria (wife of J. Murro) 90
Hall, Guillermo 135
   Jacobo Hamilton 82
   Juan 82
   Sarah 64
   Sarah Smith 82
   Tecla Ann 82
Hambley, Juan 58
Hamman, Ana (wife of E. Grove) 145
   Catalina 145
Harris, Maria 6, 83
Harrison [Herrison], Jorje 66
   Roberto 136
   Samuel 136
Hartley, Enrique 128
   Federico 63
   Francisco 129
   Guillermo 128
   Juan 62
Hassett, Thomas 3, 8, 42, 47, 90
Havero [Avero]
   Juana (wife of G. de Ita y Salazar) 84, 91
   Ursela (wife of R. de Aribas) 92

Index

Hazard, Maria (wife of M. Pery) 5, 77
Hector, Clay (wife of T. Travers) 150
Hedsorcopli, Catalina Catrinaticha 82
  Domingo 82
  Juana Hernandez 82
  Teodoro 82
Heinsman [see Hindsman]
Helzendorf [see Holzendorf]
Hendricks, Guillermo 61
  Issac 128
  Rebecca 127
Henrique (slave) 70
Henrique [Ennrique]
  Agueda (wife of J. Segui) 22, 107
  Juana Pellicer 107
  Mateo 107
Hepourth, Maria (wife of T. Carter) 106
Hernandez [Hernandes], Agueda 10
  Agueda (wife of M. Suarez) 98
  Ana Hill 116
  Angela (wife of G. Sanz) 71
  Antonio 10
  Catalina 79, 98
  Catarina 10, 24
  Diego 10, 44, 82, 98
  Dorotea Gomila 10, 79
  Gabriel 24, 98
  Gaspar 10, 79, 81, 143
  José 96, 116, 125
  Josef 45, 53, 79, 98, 124
  Joseph 10, 24
  Juan 10, 81, 98, 146
  Juana 17, 55
  Juana (wife of B. Peligri) 17, 82
  Juana (wife of D. Hedsorcopli) 82
  Juana Lina 24, 98
  Juana Ristoa 82
  Luis 148
  Magdalena (wife of E. Sanz) 96
  Magdalena (wife of E. Suarez) 96

Hernandez (cont'd)
  Magdalena Cardona 98
  Margarita 10, 79, 81
  Margarita Andreu 143
  Margarita Ponz 81
  Margarita Triay 79, 81
  Maria 24, 99
  Maria (wife of L. Cherez) 25, 99
  Maria del Carmen (wife of J. Llerena) 70
  Maria/Mariana Mier 24, 96, 98
  Maria Reyes 82
  Maria Rosa 98
  Mariana (wife of J. Pomar) 96
  Martin 10, 51, 79
  Martina 24
  Martina Victoria 98
  Micaela (wife of F. Berta) 73
  Michaela Lesana 98
  Pedro 82
  Rafael 17
  Victoria Vivas 10, 82, 98
Hernau [see Arnau]
Hester, Ana 3
  Geremias 3, 7
  Guillermo Optan 3
  Jesse 124, 126
Hibberson, Jose 141
Higginbothra, Dorotea (wife of E. Ashton) 77
Hill, Ana 108
  [see also Hull]
  Ana (wife of J. Hernandez) 116
  Antonia (wife of J. Paredes) 82
  Antonio 89
  Christina/Chrischeany 8, 108
  Deophus 7
  Donisia (wife of G. Forraster) 89
  Isabel/Isabela 8, 108
  Juan 108
  Margarita Ferrer 99

Index

Hill (cont'd)
   Maria 8, 108
   Maria del Carmen (wife of F.
     Sanchez) 108
   Maria Isabel Morlan 99
   Maria Watson 99
   Sara 7
   Sarah (wife of A. Hunter) 89
   Susanah Kean 89
   Teophilo 56, 108
   Theresa Thomasa 7, 108
   Thomas 100
Hindsman [Heinsman, Hinsman]
   Ana (wife of A. Sambias) 75
   Antonio 6, 58, 75, 101, 108
   Barbara 60
   Barbara Strasburgz/Mrasbourgh 6,
     75, 101, 108
   Catalina Antonia 108
   Ines 6
   Ines Ana Antonia 6
   Jorje 7
   Juan Jorje 7
   Leonora Genopley/Genoble 6, 108
   Lucia 108
   Margarita 6
   Maria (wife of E. Ashton) 5, 101
   Maria (wife of J. Mott) 75, 101
   Maria Barbara 6, 108
   Maria Isabela 7
Hobherk, Guillermo 146
   Sarah Fendine 146
Hocha, Josef 105
   Juana (wife of J. Ferrer) 105
   Margarita Losano 104
Hodgins [Hoggins], Daniel 64
   Ruben 63
Hollingsworth, Timoteo 60
Holmes, Isabel 65
Holzendorf, Guillermo Blunton 106
   Isabel Erhardt 106
   Isabel Rosina 106

Holzendorf (cont'd)
   Juan 106
   Juan Luis Real 106
   Federico 106
   Rosina Dupont 106
Honycutt, Agustin 77
   Francisca de Sales 77
   Maria Smith 77
Hopkins, Juan 57
   Maria (wife of F. Gudden) 72
Horit, Francisco 59, 65
Hortega [Hortegas]
   [see also de Ortegas, Ortega]
   Ana Maria Cavedo 90
   Ana Xeres 90
   Antonia (wife of P. Sabate) 99
   Bernardo 91
   Catarina 26
   Catarina Llabres 26
   Francisca 26
   Francisca Nand 104
   Ignacio 109
   Inez 91
   Lazaro 26, 109
   Maria Cherez 99
   Mariano 91
   Santiago 91
   Sebastian 90, 91, 99
Hota, Catalina (wife of R. Castillo) 114
Houghton, Maria McDonnel 72
   Patricio Gorje 72
   Thomas 72
Houston, Juan 64, 132
   Maria (wife of J. Fontanel) 115
Howard, Carlos 57
   Daniel Griffin 57
Howard y Claveria, Thimoteo 5
Hrasburgz [see Shrasburg]
Hudson, Jose
   Juan 4, 60
   Maria Evens 4
Huertas [see Guertas]

Hues [Hughes], Josef 7, 68
   Joseph 7
   Susanah Kean
Huet, Francisco 29
   [see also Guet]
   Francisco Josef 29
   Joseph Francisco 29
   Joseph Ramon 29
   Maria 29
   Maria de la Concepcion 29
   Maria Nicolasa 29
   Rosalia 29
   Rosalia Faustina 29
Hughbank, Guillermo 140
Hull
   [see also Hill]
   Antonia (wife of J. Paredes 82
   Antonio 89
   Donisia (wife of G. Forraster) 89
   Juan 99
   Pedro 99
   Sarah (wife of A. Hunter) 89
   Susanah Kean 89
Hunter, Alexandro 89
   Sarah Hill 89
   Susanah Kean 89
Hyquins, Isabel McMullen 6
   Juan 6

I

Iacens, Ana 20
Ianes [Llanes], Lorenzo 34
Ibarnau, Geronima (wife of D. del Brazo) 11
Ienocly, Juan 21
Indori, Antonia 78
   Antonia Casanovas 78
   Francisca 101
   Isabel 101
   Mariana 78
   Rafael 78

Inero, Manuela (wife of J. Galen) 92
Isabel (free Negro) 70
Isern, Agustin 114
   Isabel Mestre 114
Isnardi [Iznardy], Miguel 32, 37
Ita y Salacar [see de Ita y Salacar]

J

Jaabyt, Juliana 13
Jacome, Geronima (wife of T. Turdas) 100
Jaime (mulatto) 74
Jemison, Ana (wife of R. Andrus) 109
Jennings, Pedro 62
Jeonada [Joaneda], Antonio 101
   Francisco 15
   Juan 15, 71, 101
   Magdalena 15, 71
   Magdalena Marin 15, 71
   Magdalena Morida 101
Jinandes, Domingo 72
   Juana Torres 72
   Margarita de San Lorenzo 72
   Miguel Lorenzo 72
Johnson, Widow 63
Jomon, Isabel (wife of T. Barnet) 89
Jones, Catalina 103
   Indigo 103
   Juan 127
   Margarita Woodland 103
   Maria (wife of M. Rengil) 103
   Juan 85
   Juan Bautista 55
   Juan Bautista (slave) 73
   Juana (free Negro) 80
Junes, Thomas 3
Jurdine, Elizabeth 146, 149
Juso, Maria (wife of J. Ponz) 81
Justi, Jesse 59
Juvera, Juana (wife of B. Cintas) 71

Index

K

Kean, Guillermo 64
  Isabel (wife of A. Leslie) 79
  Juan 79
  Rebeca Pengree 79
  Susanah (wife of A. Hill) 89
Kerr, Francisca 124, 126
  Susan 149
Kevy, Barbara Bobinson 84
  Juan 84
  Josef 84
Kible, Enrique 147
  Regina Ven Fibon 147
King, Salomon 66
Kingsley, Zaphariah 129
Kunan [Coonan], Isabel (wife of G. Fitzgerald) 83
  Maria (wife of B. Wickes) 145

L

la Febre, Margarita Bohan 79
  Maria Gutreau 79
  Pedro 79
  Pedro Manuel 79
  Pheilpe Manuel 79
Laderolt, Margarita Segui 71
  Vizente 71
Ladson, Juan Conway 67
Lago, Antonia (wife of J. Fontanel) 75, 77
Lamb, Thomas 140
Lamira, Guillermo 107
  Maria Mula 107
  Pedro 107
Land, Thomas 140
Lane, Guillermo 67
  Pedro 67
Lang, Ricardo 64
Lasaga [see de Lasaga]
Lasebury, Margarita 144

Lassee, Juan 139
Later, Jorje 130
Laufrio [Llufrio], Antonia Maestre 16, 88
  Bartolomeo 16, 88
  Constantino 88
  Juan Antonio 88
  Ursula 16, 88, 142
  Ursula (wife of D. Estacholi) 142
  Ursula Alberti 88
Laurey, Juana 4
Lawrence, Ana Travers 141
  Guillermo 141
Leasewell, Maria (wife of R. Cordery) 6
Ledo, Antonio 12
Legas, Josefa (wife of C. Brabo) 115
  Maria (wife of F. Estacholy) 115
Lembras, Antonio 21
Leon, Barbara (wife of D. Estacholy) 76
Leonardi [Leonardy], Agueda Coll 14, 103
  Bartolomeo 14, 103
  Catalina Rogero 115
  Jacoba 14, 103
  Josefa Clorinda 14, 103
  Juan 14, 103, 115
  Lorenzo 148
  Margarita 103
  Maria (wife of J. Ugarte) 113
  Roque 14, 42, 49, 103
Lernen
  [see also de Gasino y Lernen],
  Ana Perren 87
  Bartolome 87
  Santiago 87
Lesana, Michaela (wife of D. Hernandez) 98
Leslie, Alexandro 79, 86
  Ana Duff 79
  Carlota 86
  Eliza 86
  Isabel Bracien 86

Index

Leslie (cont'd)
  Isabel Kean 79
  Isabel Rosa 79
  Jayme 58
  Juan 4, 58, 79
  Juana Harriot 86
  Juana Welsh 86
  Lucia 86
  Lucia Danbrooks 86
Leton, Carlos 146
  Matilde Sibbald 146
Lily, Juana 151
  William 151
Lina [Llina], Catalina (wife of R. Roger) 96
  Juan 98
  Juana (wife of J. Hernandez) 24, 98
  Juana (wife of J. Pomar) 96
  Juana Acosta 98
Lively, Maria 150
Llabres [Llebres], Antonio 26
  Catarina/Catalina 26, 109
  Catarina (wife of L. Hortegas) 26, 109
  Francisca (wife of A. Mabrumati) 28
  Jaime 109
Llama, Juan 143
Llambias [Llambrias, Sambias],
  Ana Hinsman 75
  Antonio 50, 75
  Juan 75
  Margarita Cardona 75
  Maria Sanz 75
  Pedro 26
Llanes [Llanez], Ana Resco 72
  Barbara 76
  Barbara Villegas 76
  Josef Rafael 76
  Juan 76
  Juana Albarez 76
  Lorenzo 28, 76
  Pedro 72

Llanes (cont'd)
  Phelipa (wife of J. Escalona) 72
Llerena [Llarena], Josef 70
  Juan N. V. 70
  Maria del Carmen Hernandez 70
  Maria Teresa 70
  Rita Maria 70
  Vicente 70, 147
Llesano, Margarita (wife of J. Fuchia) 107
Llina [see Lina]
Llopis [see Lopez]
Llufrio [see Laufrio]
Loftin, Juan, Jr. 62
  Juan, Sr. 62
Long, Catalina Mongumrey 76
  Christina Mathewson 76
  Gorje 76
  Mateo 76
Lopez [Lopis], Andres 10, 74, 96
  Antonia Gomez 96
  Bartolomeo 10, 50, 74
  Christobal 10, 74
  Juana 10, 74, 96
  Juana (wife of D. Namis) 142
  Juana Triay 74, 96
  Mariana Alberty 10
Lorens, Juan 53
Lorenzo, Antonio 95
  Antonia 22
  Francisco 22
  Juan 22, 95
  Juana 28, 81
  Magdalena 95
  Maria Quintana 95
  Maria Villa 22, 95
  Mariana 22, 95
  Mateo 28, 81, 95
  Margarita 105
  Paula [de] Torres 28, 81
Losano, Margarita (wife of J. Hocha) 105

Index

Low, Juan 61, 134
Lowe, Leonor (wife of F. de la Pisente) 116, 141
Lowing, Roberto 130
Luay, Juan 32
Lubera, Antonia (wife of B. Petros) 76
Lucia (free Negro) 80
Luet, Pedro 23
Luis 7, 68
Luke [Lucas], Andres 97
    Margarita Bannuche 97
    Maria 97
    Maria (wife of B. Alcina) 97
Luna, Maria (wife of J. Muse) 150
    Simon 144
Ly, Juan 7

M

Mabrite [Mabriti], Barbara Estacholy 143
    Maria (wife of J. Peso de Burgo) 78
    Maria Costa 78
    Miguel 143
    Nicolas 78
Mabrumate [Mabrumaty, Mabromaty],
    Anastacio 26, 40, 107
    Antonio 26, 40, 107
    Catalina 107
    Catarina Llabres 26
    Francisca Llabres 26, 107
    Margarita 107
    Maria 26, 107
    Maria (wife of J. Andreu) 115
    Maria Marculina 107
    Mariana 107
MacCullock, Jonathan 67
    Josef 67
MacDonald [MacDonnel, McDonald, MagDonel], Alexandro 7, 26, 59
    Almiro 72
    Ana (wife of P. Forraster) 89

MacDonald (cont'd)
    Ana (wife of A. Houghton) 72
    Brigidia (wife of P. Forraster) 89
    Ferdinand 7, 137
    Isabel 90
    Margarita Gouson 72
    Randolph 7
    Rudulfo 59
MacErones, Isabel (wife of G. McEnnis) 90
MacFeal [McTail], Margarita 73
    Margarita (wife of A. de Palma) 32, 73
    Margarita Win 73
    Paulo 73
MacGirt, Diego 56, 68
Machad, Manuel 147
Machiochi [Machoqui], Joaquin 25, 81
    Juan 25, 81
    Magdalena 25
MacLean, Isabel Page 106
    Juan 106
    Margarita (wife of H. Carter) 106
MacTail [see MacFeal]
Madan, Margarita (wife of S. Clarke) 81
Maestre [Mestre], Angela 27, 109
    Angela (wife of J. Cla) 146
    Antonia 51, 109
    Antonia (wife of B. Llufrio) 16, 88
    Antonia Roquer/Roger 13, 75, 76, 85, 88
    Antonio 13, 75
    Antony 51
    Bartolome 75, 76, 85, 88, 109
    Bartolomeo Marcelini 75
    Catalina 85
    Catalina Nickleron 75
    Catarina (wife of A. Canobas) 13, 85
    Isabel (wife of A. Isern) 114

Index

Maestre (cont'd)
  Juan 26, 109
  Maria 27, 76
  Maria (wife of M. Solana) 76, 114
  Maria Andreu/Anoreu 26, 109
  Pedro 26, 47, 109
Mall, Esperania (wife of J. Capo) 109
Malpas, Ricardo 66
Malter, Alexandro 108
  Manuel Marhal 108
  Maria Douglas 108
  Teresa Tomas 109
Manent, Juana (wife of J. Dalmedo) 99
Manney, Juana (wife of F. Triay) 142
  Margarita 144
Mans, Maria (wife of J. Blanco) 71
Manuela (slave) 70
Manusi [Maunusi], Antonia 74
  José 74, 96
  Juana Peis 96
  Juana Rio 74
  Magdalena (wife of J. Arnau) 96
Manyapany, Juana 145
Marculina, Maria (wife of A. Mabrumate) 107
Mareden [see Mureden]
Margarita (slave) 74
Margarita (free Negro) 80
Maria (free Negro) 52
Maria (slave) 18, 70
Maria Augustina (free Negro) 75
Maria del Rosario (slave) 93
Marialy, Felicia (wife of M. Bulchany) 100
Marin, Antonio 71
  Francisco 10, 21, 46, 50, 71, 85
  Juana (wife of N. Estevanoploy) 15, 83, 85
  Magdalena (wife of J. Jeoneda) 15, 71
  Magdalena Escudero 21, 71, 85

Marin (cont'd)
  Tecla (wife of E. Medochi) 71
  Tecla Casalo 71
Marinda [see Miranda]
Mars, Margarita 148
Martel, Angela Rosi 80
  Blas 80
  Gaspar 80
  Juana 80
  Juana Angela Riso 80
Martin [see Martinez], Bartolomeo 103
  Juana 103
  Juana (wife of J. Zuares) 31
  Maria Suarez 103
Martinely [Martinoly], Domingo 17, 74
  Juan 17, 74
  Maria Cavedo/Quevedo 17, 74
  Petrona 17, 74
  Petrona Povriti 74
  Santiago 17, 74
Martinez, Gregorio 104
  Isabel Soriano 104
  Juana (wife of J. Suarez) 85
  Lucia Coruna 104
  Maria Quevedo 17
  Rita Maria 104
  Martin 104
Marzail, Manuel 68
Massey, Pedro 140
Mataran, Cristiana 145
Mateor, Maria 61
Mathewson, Ana McCrey 76
  Christina (wife of G. Long) 76
  Juan 76
Maunusi [see Manusi]
Mauriri [Mauriry], Maria 19
  Maria Costa 19
  Miguel 19
Mayro, Enrique 5
  Isabela Perry 5

Index

McClure, Juan 142
McCrey, Ana (wife of J. Mathewson) 76
McCulloch, Jonathan 128
McDonald [see MacDonald]
McEnnis, Guillermo 90
   Isabel McErones 90
   Isabel Searle 90
   Juan 90
McGirt, Daniel 7
   Esacarias 7
   Isabela Sanders 7
   Jayme 7
   Juan 7
   Maria 7
   Roberto 7
McHardy, Roberto 123, 125
McIntosh, Christina Mathewson 76
   Mateo 76
   Mariana 147
   Winifred 76
McMullen, Isabel (wife of J. Hyquins) 6
McPreny, Guillermo 25
McQueen [McQuien], Ana Dalton 88
   Dayna Domingo 150
   Harry 150
   Juan 88
Medechy [Medochi, Medices],
   Antonia Pellicer 105, 115
   Elias 21, 71
   Francisco 21, 54, 71, 115
   Georje 71
   Jorje 21
   Magdalena 21
   Tecla Marin 71
Medices [see Medechy]
Medina, Catalina (wife of A. Meina) 95
Medochi [see Medechy]
Meguilson, Antonia (wife of G. Capo) 109

Meina, Antonia 95
   Antonio 95
   Catalina Alcina 95
   Catalina Medina 95
   Miguel 95
   Rafaela 95
   Rafaela Capo 95
Melia, [Mely, Mila],
   Agueda (wife of B. Villalonga) 84, 90
   Margarita (wife of L. Cardona) 90
Mely [see Melia]
Mendez, Catalina Ruiz 81
   Inez 73
   Inez Francisca (wife of J. Gomez) 81
   Lucia 81
   Maria (wife of A. Monte) 81
   Pedro 81
Menocal, Juana de Dios (wife of F. del Corral) 77
Menuce, Josef 96
   Juan 96
   Juana 96
   Juana Riso 96
   Magdalena Roque 96
   Marcos 96
   Pedro 96
Mercadal, Rafaela (wife of H.Villalonga) 22
Mestre [see Maestre]
Mexias, Vicente 88
Meyerhoven, Margarita R. 57
Miller, Samuel 127
Mills, Josef 68
Mintero, Maria de Cordoba 93
   Melchora (wife of V. Moreno) 93
   Pedro 93
Mir [Mier], Catalina 73
   Catalina (wife of J. Solano) 142
   Catalina Pom 98
   Catalina/Catarina 18, 73

Index

Mir (cont'd)
  Gabriel 98
  Juana (wife of A. Escudero) 71
  Maria/Mariana (wife of J. Hernandez) 24, 98
  Mariana Zans 73
  Michaela 18, 73
Miranda [Marinda, Mirando], Antonia 87
  Diego 74, 79, 87
  Francisco Xavier 79
  Juana Margarita Ribero 74, 79, 87
  Maria (wife of A. Almansa) 87
  Maria Andrea Sanchez 79
  Maria de la Concepcion 87
  Maria de los Dolores (wife of R Dias) 74
  Maria Juliana Ramona 79
  Maria Manuela 79
  Maria Sanchez 112
  Pedro 87, 112
  Pedro Josef 87
  Silvestre 87
Mongumrey, Catalina (wife of M. Long) 76
  Maria (wife of T. Tomson) 96
Monte, Alexander 81
  Felix Josef 81
  Josef Antonio 81
  Maria Mendez 81
Montes de Oca, Antonio 28, 34, 81
  Antonio Joseph 32
  Bartolome 81
  Christostimo 102
  Josefa 81
  Josefa Rodriguez 81
  Juana (wife of C. Gonzales) 29, 34, 102
  Leonarda Josefa 32
  Paula de Tores 28, 81
Mora/Moore Isabela/ Isavel (wife of F. Segui) 18

Moreno, Antonio 87, 93
  Catalina Suarez 93
  Feranando Maria 93
  Melchora Mintero 93
  Josefa (wife of F. Beltido) 85
  Juan de la Crux 93
  Juana 95
  Juana F. 95
  Maria Manuela 93
  Nicolas Agustin 93
  Ramon 93
  Vicente 93
Morida, Margarita (wife of A. Joaneda) 101
Morilla, Antonia (wife of J. Tenevardy) 21
Morlan, Francisco 99
  Maria Isabel 99
Morrison, Miguel 75
  Mrs. 75
  Rosa 75
Mory, Ricardo 4
  Richeld Blent 4
Mott, Ana 101
  Antonio 101
  Bernardo 16
  Ines 5
  Isabela 5, 75, 101
  Isabela (wife of J. Arnau) 5
  Jonas 75
  Maria Hinsman 5, 75, 101
Mrasbourgh [see Shrasburg]
Mula, Bernado 86
  Catalina Villa 86
  Isabela (wife of J. Arnau) 13, 86
  Maria (wife of M. Hernau) 107
  Maria (wife of C. Sanz) 107
Mulcartre, Sarah (wife of T. Ellerbee) 79
Mureden, Ana 108

Index

Mureden (cont'd)
   Edwardo 100
   Inez 100
   Juana Daly 75
   Maria Ana 100
   Martin 100
   Sarah Nelson 100
Murro, Guillermo 90
   Hana 90
   Jorje 90
   Maria (wife of C. Dominguez) 115
   Maria Hacket 90
Muse, Juan 150
   Maria Luna 150

N

Namis, Damion 142
   Juana Lopez 142
Nand, Francisca (wife of L. Hortegas) 109
Navarra [Navarre, Navarro],
   Francisco 28
   Isabel F. (wife of B. Suarez) 103
   Juana (wife of S. de Porras) 93
   Miguel 96
Nelson, Ambrosio 67
   Hana Wilson 100
   Reason 100
   Sarah (wife of M. Mureden) 100
Neto [see Nielo]
Nickleron, Catalina (wife of A. Mestre) 75
   Guillermo 75
   Juana Daly 75
Nicoliche [Nicolik, Nicholiche]
   Josepha Coll 19, 100
   Manuela 19, 100
   Maria 100
   Maria Tarrabuche 100

Nicoliche (cont'd)
   Martin 19, 100
   Nicolas 19, 100
   Rafaela 100
Nielo, Clara Victorina 108
   Juan 108
   Margarita (wife of J. Salon) 14, 108
Nifuelas, Catalina (wife of F. Entargo) 87
   Catalina Cantal 87
   Josef 87
Nixon, Ana 88
   Ana Ursula Andrade 88
   Inharia 88
   Isabel (wife of J. Ferrreyna) 88
   Juan 88
Noble, Duncan 4, 59
Norwart, Catalina (wife of G. Bracien) 86
Notachisa, Marta (wife of T. Coufacio) 77

O

O'Brien, Maria (wife of E. Parkinson) 84, 102
O'Callaghan, Bernardo 76
Ogden, Barney 97
   Maria Cousons 97
   Moyses 97
Olard, Juan 102
   Margarita 102
   Margarita Anastacia 102
   Maria 102
Olibas [Olivas], Eulalia (wife of F. Bausa) 13
   Francisca (wife of J. Ridavets) 82
   Maria (wife of M. Segui) 109
Oliberas [Olibera, Oliveras],
   Antonio 37
   Catalina 95

Index

Oliberas (cont'd)
  Catalina 95
  Catalina (wife of A. Alberti) 10, 95
  Catalina (wife of A. Gavardy) 10,101
  Maria (wife of A. Andreu) 95
O'Neil, Enrique 63
O'Reilly, Father 46, 48, 55, 67, 83
  Juan 83
  Lorenzo 83
  Miguel 60, 83
Ormand, Manuel 126
  R. 124, 126
Ortega [Ortegas],
  [see also de Ortegas, Hortegas]
  Ana 109
  Ana Maria 16
  Ana Maria Quevedo 16
  Antonia 72
  Antonia (wife of P. Sabalt) 23
  Bernardo 16
  Catalina 109
  Catalina Llebres 109
  Francisca 109
  Francisca Nand 109
  Francisco 72
  Ignacia Antonia 72
  Ignacio 32, 37, 109
  Josef 92
  Josefa (wife of S. Garcia) 92
  Juana N. 72
  Lazaro 109
  Lorenzo 49
  Maria (wife of P. Osias) 23, 99
  Maria Castaneda 92
  Maria Josefa 72
  Santiago 16
  Sevastian 16
Osias, Ana 23, 99
  Ana Cristiana 99
  Geronimo 99
  Maria 99
  Maria Ortegas 23, 99

Osias (cont'd)
  Pedro 23
  Sebastian 99
  Ozana, Jina 150

P

Pablo, Inez (wife of J. Clak) 24
Paceti [Pacety, Pascety],
  Andres 17, 42, 89
  Andres Daecte 17
  Antonio 42
  Benita 92
  Bartolomeo 89
  Clara 141
  Clara (wife of D. Carreras) 89
  Clara Maria 17
  Francisca 73
  Gaspar 15
  Getrudis 89, 141
  Getrudis Ponz 89
  Getrudis R. 17
  Magdalena 17, 89
  Maria Castel 17, 89
  Thomas 17, 89
Padron, Francisca (wife of J. Guadarama) 73
Page, Isabel (wife of J. McLean) 106
Pallicer [Pellicier, Pallerin],
  Antonia 105
  Antonia (wife of F. Medices) 105, 115
  Antonia Morilla 21
  Antonio 19, 76, 105
  Benita (wife of B. Alcina) 97
  Francisco 19, 76, 84, 105, 114
  Juan Antonio 105
  Juana 19, 107
  Juana (wife of M. Henrique) 107
  Juana (wife of A. Ximenes) 84
  Juana Cintas 105

Index

Pallicer (cont'd)
   Juana Villa 19, 84, 105, 114
   Magdalena (wife of P. Ponz) 98
   Margarita (wife of P. Escobal) 97
   Margarita Femenias 76
   Maria 19, 20, 105
   Martin 21
Palma [see de Palma]
Papi [Papy, Popee], Ana 85
   Ana Pons 15, 85, 111
   Catalina 85
   Catalina (wife of F. Solano) 113
   Catalina Auas 85
   Gaspar 15, 42, 85, 111, 103
   Maria 85
   Maria (wife of D. Reyes) 114
   Miguel 85
Paredes, Antonia Hill 82
   Isabel Ridavetes 82
   Josef 82
   Juan 82
   Juana 82
   Margarita 82
   Margarita Ensenada 82
   Ramon 82
Parish, Juan 5, 57
Parkinson, Edwardo 84
   Juan 84
   Maria O'Brien 84, 102
Parla, Catalina Brass 91
   Juan 91
   Maria (wife of D. Tudelache) 91
   Maria (wife of D. Costa) 91
Pasceti [see Pacety]
Pasqual, Margarita (wife of J. Arnau) 144
Pasquo, Pedro 41
Pau, Jaimio 52
Paulo, Inez (wife of P. Duran) 109
Payeres, Isabela Ridabet 12
   Juan Bautista 12
   Juana 12

Paz, Francisco 111
Peabet, Mr. 57
Pedro de Burgo [see Peso de Burgo]
Peis, Juana (wife of J. Maunusi) 96
Pelegrin [see Pelegrino]
Pellegrino [Peligri, Pelegrin, Peregrin],
   Ana Maria 25
   Ana Maria Triay 101
   Antonia 17, 82
   Bartolomeo 76
   Fernando 25
   Juana 82
   Juana Hernandez 17, 82
   Maria 13, 25, 76, 101
   Maria (wife of F. Estacholi) 13, 76
   Matheo 25, 101
Peligir [see Pellegrino]
Pellicer [see Pallicer]
Peluda, Magdalena (wife of B. Segui) 107
Pemberton, Jorje 68
   Thomas 68
Pengree, Guillermo 62, 66
   Rebecca (wife of J. Kean) 79
Pepall [see Perpal]
Pepino 49
Pepod, Isabel Pras y 16
Perdomo, Antonia (wife of F. Aredondo) 94
   Ignacio 94
   Nicolsa Gomez 94
Peregrin [see Pellegrino]
Perez, Antonia (wife of D. Cuello) 75
   Bartolomeo 101
   Beatriz de la Rosa 101
   Francisco 147
   Jose 143
   Juana 28
   Juana (wife of J. Sanchez) 108
   Juana de la Rosa 71
   Luisa (wife of M. de Almanza) 101
   Maria Beatris Sanchez 147

Index

Perpal [Perpall, Pepal], Domingo 16
   Gabriel 16, 124, 126
   Isabel 52
   Isabel Pras y Pepld 16
   Juan 16
   Juana 16
   Margarita (wife of J. Carreras) 82
   Maria Garcia (wife of T. de Aribas) 16, 92
Perry [Pery, Peny], Isabela 5
   Isabela 5
   Maria 5
   Maria (wife of R. de Fuentes) 77, 114
   Maria Hazard 5, 77
   Marmaduke 77
Peso de Burgo, Domingo 94
   Geronima Camugina 78
   Josef 78
   Joseph 12, 30
   Lucia 9, 54, 94
   Magdalena de Nuncio 94
   Maria Mabriti 78
   Pedro 9, 78, 94, 144
   Pedro Josef Antonio 78
   Pepino 47
Petarson, Juan 150
Petros, Antonia 14
   Antonia Lubera 76
   Bartolomeo 76
   Maria (wife of F. Stacoly/Estacholi) 13, 76
Petty, Juan 129
Pevet, Mistress 51
Pietos [see Pretos]
Piket [Picot], Flora Celia 113
   Maria Rebeca 148
   Seymond 148
Piles, Ana (wife of J. Smith) 82
Pilot, Diego 137
Piumbi, Rosa (wife of M. Buchantini) 74

Plummer [Plomer], Daniel 66
   Susana 129
Pom, Catalina (wife of G. Mir), 98
Pomar, Josef 96
   Juan 96
   Juana (wife of M. Figuera) 97
   Juana Lina 96
   Maria Hernandez 96
Pomas, José 148
Pon, Agata 18, 91
Poncella, Francisca 13
   Maria Magdalena 13
Ponells, Antonia (wife of F. Arnau) 94
Pons [Ponz]
   [see also Pom, Pon, Ponz de Leon]
   Agueda 18
   Agueda (wife of A. Andres) 11, 98
   Agueda Euget 91
   Ana 111
   Ana (wife of G. Papi) 15, 85, 111
   Antonia 18, 91
   Antonia Triay 23
   Antonio 95, 97, 148
   Barbara (wife of J. Ximinez) 92
   Bartolomeo 148
   Benita Alcina 97
   Catalina 70
   Catarina (wife of J. Arnau/Andreu) 27, 109
   Clara (wife of J. Fornalis) 85
   Dimas 78
   Francisca (wife of S. Coll) 99, 17
   Francisca (wife of P. Furnelles) 78
   Francisca Coll 85, 107, 109
   Francisco 11, 18, 44, 78, 91
   Getrudiz (wife of A. Pasceti) 89
   Getrudis Carreras 141
   Jose 82
   Josef 48, 69, 78
   Josef de Triay 48

Index

Pons (cont'd)
   Josefa (wife of R. Leonardy) 103
   Josefa (wife of I. Vadel) 82
   Josefa (wife of B. Coll) 100
   Joseph 9
   Juan 54, 81, 95, 102
   Juan F. 81
   Juan Triay 23
   Juana 11, 98, 108
   Juana (wife of A.Caulas) 93
   Juana (wife of J. Triay) 92
   Juana (wife of M. Salom) 108
   Juana Andrea 25
   Juana Villa 18, 91
   Manuel 18
   Magdalena (wife of J. Machoqui) 81
   Magdalena Pallicer 98
   Margarita 25, 97
   Margarita (wife of J. Hernandez) 81
   Margarita (wife of G. Triay) 24
   Margarita Cardona 95
   Margarita Redavetes 81, 102
   Maria 97
   Maria Capella 78
   Maria Juso 81
   Maria Triay 78
   Mariana 95
   Mariana Rugera 9, 69
   Mathias 40, 91
   Miguel 85, 109
   Pedro 91, 98, 141
Pons de [y] Triay [see Triay],
   Dimas 12
   Josef 48
   Joseph 12
   Margarita Triay 12
Ponz [see Pons]
Ponz de Leon
   Catalina de Porras 93
   Ciriaco 93
   Francisco 93

Ponz de Leon (cont'd)
   Jacoba Puello 93
   Josef 93
   Joseph 12
   Manuela 93
   Rosalia (wife of J. del Toro) 72
Pool, Isril 137
Popee [see Papi]
Posill, Antonio 19
   Mariana Fuesliny 19
Povriti, Petrona (wife of J. Martinely) 74
Powel, Josef 80
   Juan 80
   Sarah Clapton 80
Prado, Maria de los Agelos (wife of T.
   Bravo) 83
Prais [Pras], Francisco 12
   Jayme 49
   Isabela y Pepod 16
Pramas, Nancy 150
Pras y Pepod [see Pepod]
Prast, Margarita Vivas 19
   Santiago 19
Pratt [Pratts], Francisca (wife of S.
   Pretos) 21, 94
   Francisco 91
   Jaime 91
   Maria Campos 91
   Margarita Vivos 91
Preites [Preta, Pretos, Pritos],
   Clara (wife of F. Arnau) 94, 21
   Francisca 107
   Francisca (wife of P. Fuchia/Fezua)
      22, 107
   Jaime 107
   Margarita 107
   Margarita (wife of T. Andreu) 27
   Maria (wife of J. Cla) 98
   Santiago 94, 107
Preta [see Preites]
Pue, Luiz 103

Index

Pue (cont'd)
  Margarita 103
  Williby 103
Puella [Puello, Pueyo], Antonio 29, 36, 42
  Francisco 15, 47
  Jacoba (wife of F. Ponz de Leon) 93
  Maria Manuela 29
Pueyo [see Puella]
Puima, Isabel (wife of L. Rodriguez) 29, 79, 80, 86, 87, 102
  Maria 79, 86
Pule, Mariana 150
Pullares, Juan Antonio 38
Purcel, Antonia 78
  Isabela Druly 80
  Jaime 80
  Juan 80
  Mariana Indori 78
Purla, Inez (wife of J. Cla) 98
  Mariana Rodriguez 98
  Pedro 98

Q

Quemana, Ana (wife of A. Triay) 96
Quesada, Sebastiana (wife of A. Cortes) 102
Quevedo [see Cavio], Ana Maria (wife of A. Triay) 16
  Ines (wife of P. Coufacio) 17
  Juan 15
  Juana Seguy 15
  Mariana (wife of D. Martinoly) 17
Quinomez, Antonia (wife of M. Cescaloma) 84
Quintana, Ana (wife of P. Estopa) 25
  Ana (wife of A. Triay) 97
  Juana (wife of J. Funelles) 78
  Mariana (wife of J. Lorenzo) 95
  Matheo 97

Quintero, Elvira (wife of J. de Palma) 73
Qunada, Yima (Yuna?) 50

R

Rabel, Rosa (wife of M. Navarro) 96
Rafael (slave) 94
Rains, Josef 63
  Thomas
Ramalera [Ramillera], Domingo 93
  Esparansa Campos 93
  Maria (wife of R. Ximenes) 20, 93
  Ramon 96
Ramos, Agueda Vera 86
  Melchora (wife of J. Aguilar) 33, 86, 103, 112
  Thomas 86
Redevetes [Redavetes, Ridavetes], Catalina (wife of V. Casaly) 79, 85
  Francisca Olivas 82
  Isabel (wife of J. Paredes) 82
  Juan 82
  Juana (wife of A. Canobas) 85
  Margarita (wife of J. Ponz) 82, 102
Redondo, Margarita (wife of F. Blas) 32
Rengil, Catalina Batuarte 103
  Ignacio 103
  Manuel 103
  Maria Jones 103
  Miguel 103
Rentey, Felix 143
Resco, Ana (wife of P. Llanes) 72
Reu, Alonso 71
  Antonia (wife of B. Cintas) 71
  Margarita Alcina 71
Revi, Antonio 46
Reyes, Catarina 22
  Cristoval 22
  Domingo 80, 114
  Francisco 80

Index

Reyes (cont'd)
  Gabril 80
  José 113
  Josef 80
  Juan 10, 22, 82
  Juana Maria Albertiny 22, 82
  Manuela Belen Chacon 80
  Maria 151
  Maria Luisa Riso 80
  Maria Papy 114
  Maria Seguy 113
  Mariana 22
  Mariana (wife of D. Hernandez) 82
Ribero [see Rivero]
Richard, Ribeca 127
Ridabet, Isabela (wife of J. B. Payeres) 12
Ridavetes [see Redavetes]
Rima, Juan 24
  Jorje 24
Rio [Rios, Rioas], Ana Maria 151
  Isach 65
  Jayme 151
  Jorje 96
  Juana (wife of J. Manusi) 74
  Maria Antonia 144
Riso, Antonia Castel 96
  Isach 65
  Juana (wife of J. Menuce) 96
  Juana Angela (wife of B. Martel) 80
  Manuela Chacon 80
  Marcos 96
  Maria Luisa (wife of G. Reyes) 80
  Pedro 96
  Pedro Antonio 96
Ristoa, Juana (wife of P. Hernandez) 82
Rite, Maria 150
Rivas, Isabel 151
  Joseph A. 28
  Nancy 151
Rivera [Riveras, Rivero]
  Adefonso Josef 36
  Alfonzo 28

Rivera (cont'd)
  Antonio 32
  Francisco 87
  Isabel Rodriguez 87
  Juana Margarita (wife of D. Miranda) 74, 79, 87, 97
Roch [Roche], Ana Barnet 89
  Clara 89
  Francisca 32, 89
  Francisco 32, 38, 89
  Josef 89
  Margarita Barnet 32, 89
  Roberto 46
Rodrigues[z], Alecia Wedington 75
  Ana Maria Escobal 79
  Catalina Ruiz 82
  Catalina Zuares 31
  Dionisia (wife of B. Segui) 86, 113
  Domingo de Leon 61
  Domingo Rafael 86
  Francisca 71, 83
  Francisca (wife of F. Carilla) 83
  Francisca Aguilar 86
  Isabel (wife of M. Entargo) 87
  Isabel (wife of F. Rivera) 87
  Isabela Casimira (wife of M. Romero) 80
  Isabela Casildy Puima 29, 79–80, 86–87
  Joaquin 34
  Josefa (wife of B. Montes de Oca) 81
  Josefa Ruiz 86
  Juan 43, 86
  Lorenzo 29, 38, 79–80, 82, 86–87, 102
  Manuel 31, 86
  Maria (wife of J. Acosta) 104
  Maria (wife of P. Gomez) 81, 97
  Maria 81, 104
  Maria del Carmen (wife of S. Venazulace) 29, 87
  Maria Getrudiz (wife of P. Gomez) 94

Index

Rodrigues (cont'd)
  Maria Luisa (wife of P. Tontanel) 5, 75
  Maria Rafaela (wife of M. Bendicho) 80
  Maria Rafaela Scott 86
  Mariana (wife of P. Purla) 98
  Nicolas 29, 86
  Pedro 11, 38, 79, 82
  Simon 75
  Theresa de Jesus 29, 102
  Thomas 86
Rogaya, Juan 37
Roger [Rogero, Rogier, Roguer]
  Alberto 24, 25, 96
  Ana 76
  Antonia 13, 88, 96
  Antonia (wife of B. Maestre) 13, 75 76, 85, 88
  Antonia Villa 24, 75
  Antono 75
  Catalina 24, 25, 96
  Catalina (wife of J. Leonardy) 115
  Catalina Lina 96
  Juan 70
  Magdalena (wife of M. Menuce) 96
  Margarita 70
  Margarita (wife of L. Capella) 70
  Margarita Arnau 70
  Maria 96
  Mariana 25, 84
  Ramon 24, 96
Rolan, Juan 42
Romero, Isabel Casimira Rodriguez 80
  Juan Francisco 80
  Manuel 80
  Manuel Mauricio 80
  Paula Plutarca 80
Ronfrin, Bartholomeo 48
Roquer [see Roger]
Ros, Pedro 71

Rosa (slave) 13
Rosario, Clara (wife of M. Segui) 18, 71
Rosi [Rossi, Rosy] Angela 80
  Angela (wife of G. Martel) 9
  Catalina 71
  Francisca 9, 71
  Francisca Sanz 71, 80
  Francisco 71
  Gaspar 9, 71, 148
  Joseph 9, 49, 71, 80
  Juana 80
  Margarita 9, 143
  Margarita Salti 71
  Matilda Flora 147
  Pedro 71
Rosollo [see Rosario]
Rospain, Antonio 31
Rosy [see Rosi]
Royo, Antonia 25
  Antonio 25
Ruez [Ruis, Ruez], Catalina (wife of L. Rodriguez) 82
  Catalina (wife of P. Mendez) 81
  Catalina del Camo 81
  Josef 86
  Maria (wife of J. Soche) 93
Ruger [see Roger]
Rugera [Ruquera, Roguera; see Roger]
  Ana Maria 69
  Isabel Arnau 69
  Josefa de Troya y (wife of F. de Almanza) 101
  Magdalena 9, 96
  Maria 93
  Maria Ana (wife of J. Pons) 8, 69
  Mariana (wife of G. Venz) 69
  Mariana 9
  Santiago 69
Ruis, Ruiz [see Ruez]
Rupir, Luisa (wife of A. Guertas) 103

Index

Rusken, Juan 150
Russell, Juan 148

S

Sabalt [Sabate], Ana 99
   Antonia Ortegas 23, 99
   Catalina 99
   Catalina Capo 99
   Catarina 23
   Miguel 23, 99
   Pablo 23, 99
   Sebastina 99
Sabatier, Pablo 46
Saby, Joseph 61
Sahabedra, Antonio Gonzales 102
   Agustina Espinosa 102
   Augustine de los Monteros 102
   Maria Gonzales 102
   Rafaela Espinosa 102
   Roberto 102
   Thomas 102
Salada, Nicloas 45
Salazar [see de Ita y Salacar]
Salon [Salom, Solon], Clara 14, 108
   Juan 14, 42, 108
   Juana 108
   Juana (wife of F. Esteves) 14, 108
   Juana Ponz 108
   Margarita 108
   Margarita Neto/Nielo 14, 108
   Miguel 108
Salti, Margarita (wife of P. Rosi) 71
Salzedo, Maria Galen 92
   Pedro Josef 92
Sambias [see Llambias]
San Lorenzo [see de San Lorenzo]
Sanchez, Agueda 78, 117
   Ana 78
   Ana (wife of J. Ferrer) 78
   Antonia 143
   Antonia Espinosa 70, 79

Sanchez (cont'd)
   Antonio 78
   Bernardino 28
   Catalina de Soto 91
   Catalina Rosa 78
   Diego 83
   Felicia (wife of F. Embara) 117
   Francisca 148
   Francisca Acosta 83
   Francisco 30, 39-40, 108, 109
   Francisco Mateo 30, 78
   Francisco Xavier 35, 78
   Joaquin 83, 116
   José 83, 116, 151
   Josef 70, 78-79, 83, 108
   Josefa 146
   Joseph 28
   Juan 91
   Juan Bautista 117
   Juan Josef 83
   Juana (wife of J. de Salas) 102
   Juana de la Rosa 83
   Juana Perez 108
   Lucia (wife of J. Garcia) 104
   Manuel 108
   Manuela (wife of J. Coruna) 31
   Maria 28, 91, 146
   Maria (wife of F. Dewy) 146
   Maria (wife of J. Garcia) 92
   Maria Andres 28
   Maria Andrea/Andres (wife of F. Miranda) 79
   Maria Beatris (wife of F. Perez) 78, 147
   Maria Castenada 91
   Maria de la Concepcion 78
   Maria de la O. 28, 70
   Maria del Carmen 78
   Maria del Carmen Hill 108
   Maria Rita Bravo 83, 116
   Nicolas 28, 70
   Rafaela 108

Index

Sanchez (cont'd)
  Ramon 28, 70
  Xavier 78
Sanco, Domingo 150
  Gres 150
Sander [Sanders, Saunders],
  Guillermo 136
  Isabela (wife of J. McGirt) 7
  Juan 104
Sangarote 89
Sans [Sanz, Zans], Antonia Fernaris 11
  Angela Hernandez 71
  Cosme 107
  Esteban 73
  Estevan 96
  Francisca 71, 80
  Francisca (wife of J. Rosi) 71
  Gaspar 71
  Juana 11
  Magdalena Hernandez 96
  Margarita (wife of G. Triay) 96
  Maria (wife of G. Lamira) 107
  Maria/Mariana (wife of A. Berta) 18, 73
  Maria (wife of B. Arnau) 26, 107
  Micaela Hernandez 73
  Pasqual 11
Sante, Pasqual 43
Sardina, Josefa (wife of J. Artiles) 104
Sasgarse, Maria Josefa (wife of F. Aguirre) 88
Saunders [see Sanders]
Sceret, Maria (wife of P. Dulzet) 74
Scott, Juan 86
  Maria Rafaela (wife of N. Rodriguez) 86
  Rafaela 86
  Sarah Briton 86
Searle, Isabel (wife of J. McEnnis) 90
Seguera, Agueda (wife of J. Capo) 26, 87

Segui [Seguy], Agata 17
  Agata Maria 18
  Agueda 14, 82, 89
  Agueda (wife of J. Capo) 109
  Agueda (wife of B. Castel) 82, 89
  Agueda (wife of D. Cortes) 102
  Agueda Henrique 22, 107
  Agueda Villalonga 14, 84, 90, 102
  Ana Maria de los Dolores (wife of P. de Cala) 95, 112
  Antonia 14, 84, 107
  Antonia (wife of B. Castro y Ferrer) 112
  Bartolomeo 14, 84
  Benito 22, 107
  Bernardo 14, 53, 84, 90, 102, 113
  Blanca 14, 84
  Blanca (wife of E. Gomez) 113
  Catalina 82, 107
  Clara 14, 18, 84
  Clara Rosario/Rosollo 18, 71
  Diego 11, 53, 74, 82, 145
  Dionosia Rodriguez 113
  Domingo 27, 44, 107
  Francisca 18
  Francisco 18, 36,
  Gabriel 43
  Guillermo 100
  Isabel 95
  Isabela Mora 18
  Juan 11, 18, 22, 44, 82, 89, 95, 107
  Juana 11, 18, 82, 90, 100, 143
  Juana (wife of J. Candelaria) 144
  Juana (wife of J. Cavio/Cabedo) 15, 90
  Juana Alcina 84
  Juana Castel 11, 74, 82
  Juana Maria 18
  Lorenzo 84
  Magdalena 18, 100
  Magdalena Campino 100
  Magdalena Peluda 18, 107

Index

Segui (cont'd)
    Margarita 18, 27, 71, 107
    Margarita (wife of V. Laderolt) 74
    Maria 11, 84
    Maria (wife of J. Reyes) 113
    Maria Castel 17, 89
    Maria Ferrer 82
    Maria Olibas 109
    Maria Rosa (wife of J. Barber) 74
    Matheo 22
    Miguel 18, 43, 71, 100, 109
    Nicolas 18, 100
Seropoly, Domingo 54
Sharp, Juan 147
    Mary Vincent 147
Shasburgh [Strasburg; Mrashburg],
    Barbara (wife of A. Hindsman) 6, 75, 108
Sibbald, Carlos 149
    Matilde 146
    Rebeca (wife of F. Bethune) 149
Sientes, Bartholomeo 9
    Magdalena Rugera 9
Silva, Gregoria (wife of A. de Fuentes) 77
Simpson, Ana 6
    Barbara Jaysman 6, 58
    Felipe 6
    Guillermo 61
Sims, Thomas 63
Slop
    [see also Estopa]
    Juana Barcelo 92
    Maria (wife of F. Triay) 92
    Pedro 92
Smith, Ana Dawrino 108
    Ana Piles 82
    Catalina 108
    Diego 139
    Guillermo 108
    Jacobo 82

Smith (cont'd)
    Juan 102, 108
    Maria (wife of A. Honycutt) 77
    Sarah (wife of J. Hall) 82
    Thomas 108
Sobauch, Maria Elizabeth 144
Soche [Sochis], Antonia Tremol 24, 93
    Juan 93
    Luis 24, 46, 93
    Maria Ruiz 93
Solana [Salano], Bartolomeo 76
    Catalina Mir 142
    Catalina Papy 113
    Felipe 113
    Geronima Cerano 76
    Juan 143
    Lorenzo 76
    Manuel 36, 59, 76, 114
    Maria Maestre 76, 114
    Phelipe 76
    Ramona (wife of S. Fernandez) 102
Solon [see Salon]
Soriano, Isabel (wife of G. Martinez) 104
Stacoly [see Estacholy]
Stefanopoly [see Estefanopoly]
Sterrats, Guillermo 141
    Maria 11
Stone, Maria Beatriz 78
Stopa [see Estopa]
Stormes, Tomas 146
Strasburgh [see Shrasburg]
Suarez, Agueda Casaly 85
    Agueda Hernandez 98
    Antonio 136
    Bartolome 31, 85, 103
    Catalina (wife of A. Moreno) 93
    Francisco 98
    Gregorio 31, 103
    Isabel Navarro 103
    Josef 31, 103

Index

Suarez (cont'd)
  Juan 31, 85, 103
  Juana (wife of R. Gonzales) 81
  Juana Martinez/Martin 31, 85, 103
  Manuel 33, 98
  Maria (wife of B. Martin) 103
  Rosa de Lias 98
  Ursula (wife of P. Coruna) 104
Suau, Jeronima (wife of M. Capella) 109
Sulivan, Jesse 124, 126
Sumerland, Josef 64
Summeral, Jose 128
  Sarah 129
Sweeny [Swiney], 126
  Daniel 124
  Enrique 127

T

Tabares, Antonio 148
Tarrabuche, Maria (wife of M. Nicoliche) 106
Tate (Teats), Diego 56
  Jayme 6
  Juan 4
Taylor, Juan 9, 48
Teats, Jayme 6
  Juan 4
Tedulache [see Tudelache]
Tenevardy, Antonia Morilla 21
  Francisco 21
  Juan 21
  Juana 21
  Margarita 21
  Maria Antonia 21
Terradas, Mateo 143
Terri, Juan 53
Thomas (free Negro) 52
Thomas (slave) 73

Thomas [Tomas, Tomasa, Thomasa],
  Christina 108
  Juan 108
  Teresa 115, 144
  Teresa (wife of T. Hill) 7, 108
  Teresa (wife of D. Malter) 108, 144
Tompson [Tomson], Maria (wife of M. Navarro) 96
  Maria Mongumrey 96
  Roefulfo 65
  Thomas 96
Toranter, Juan 69
Tordo [Turdo], Joseph 12
Torres [see also de Tores]
  Bernardo 81
  Catalina Bernal 72
  Josefa (wife of D. Espinosa) 70
  Juana (wife of M. Jinandes) 72
  Juana Capman 81
  Paula (wife of A. Montes de Oca) 81
  Rafael 72
Travers [Travies], Aaron 66, 129
  Ana 83, 141
  Ana (wife of G. Lawrence) 141
  Ana Carrel 83
  Clay Hector 150
  Guillermo 66
  Jayme 66
  Juan 83
  Margarita 141
  Maria 83, 141
  Maria Fitzgerald 83
  Thomas 83
  Torry 150
Treal [Trual]
  Maria (wife of J. Espineta) 20, 93
  Magdalena del Pozo 93
  Maria (wife of J. Triay) 82
  Sebastian 93
Trean, Guillermo 76
  Margarita Geynon 76

Index

Trean (cont'd)
  Maria Ana 76
Tremol, Ana Maria (wife of M.
    Peregrino) 100
  Antonia (wife of L. Soche) 24, 93
  Francisco 24
  Margarita Campos 93
  Pedro 93
Triay
  [see also Pons de (y) Triay]
  Ana 96
  Ana Quintana 96
  Ana Turan 25
  Antonia 100
  Antonia (wife of M. Gomez) 96
  Antonia (wife of J. Pons) 23
  Antonia Campos 78
  Antonio 23, 24, 96
  Barbara 92
  Catarina Duran 25
  Francisco 19, 20, 43, 92, 142
  Gabriel 24, 96
  Guillermo 20
  Josef 82
  Juan 20, 47, 50, 78, 92, 148
  Juana 23, 96, 99, 148
  Juana (wife of A. Lopez) 74, 96
  Juana (wife of A. Tudoni) 99
  Juana Manney 142
  Juana Ximenes 20, 92
  Margarita (wife of J. Pons y Triay) 12
  Margarita (wife of G. Hernandez) 79, 81
  Margarita Pons 24
  Margarita Sans 96
  Maria 19, 92
  Maria (wife of J. Ponz) 78
  Maria (wife of J. Carreras) 22, 82, 89
  Maria Alberty 100
  Maria Englada 92

Triay (cont'd)
  Maria Slop 92
  Maria Trual (Treal) 82
  Miguel 100
  Pedro 25, 48, 100
Trual [see Treal]
Trutilon, Josef 99
  Juana Gomez 99
  Luis 99
  Maria Ana Vidata 99
Tucker, Ezekiah 140
Tudelache [Tudidache, Tudichy]
  Antonio 20, 45
  Dometrio 20, 40, 91
  Maria Braus 20
  Maria Parla 91
  Nicolas 20, 91
Tudoni, Agustin 99
  Antonia 99
  Antonia (wife of M. Gomez) 99
  Juana Triay 99
Turan, Ana 25
  Gabriel 25
Turdas [Tundas], Geronima 100
  Geronima Jacome 100
  Jose 100
  Maria Gavardy 100
  Thomas 100
  Maria Gavardy 100
  Thomas 100
Turday [Furday], Josef 41

U

Uberty, Juana 150
Ugarte, Jose M. 113
  Maria Leonardy 113
Urbino, Maria 106

V

Vadel, Ise 82

──────────────────────────── Index

'adel (cont'd)
  Josefa Pons 82
  Pedro 82
'aldez, Maria Aniceta 74
'alencia, Vicentt 142
'alez [Velez], Bernardo 73
  Domingo 20, 93
  Francisca Gomez 73
  Juana Andreu 93
  Manuel 73
als [Bals], Domingo 11, 20, 93
  Juana Andrea 20, 93
anazulace [see Venazulace]
aughan, Juan 138
ega, Antonia 31
  Catalina Zuares 31
  Joaquin 31
ell, Margarita 150
elory, Margarita (wife of F. Falany) 9, 105
en Fibon, Regina (wife of E. Kible) 147
enazulace [Vanazulace], Isabella 87
  Juan 87
  Manuel 87
  Manuela 87
  Maria del Carmen Rodrigues 87
  Maria Esperania 87
  Sebastian 87
enent, Prarides (wife of A. Canter) 78
ens [see Venz]
entura, Maria Delgad 147
enz [Vens], Ana Ferrer 99
  Ana Maria 99
  Antonia 9, 69
  Antonia (wife of G. Alvarez) 9, 69
  Catarina (wife of V. Carelli) 15
  Guillermo 69
  Josef 99
  Juana 99
  Juana (wife of F. del Medo) 22
  Mariana Rugera/Roquera 9, 69

Venz (cont'd)
  Pedro 99
Vera [Veri], Agueda (wife of T. Ramos) 86
  Ana (wife of J. Capella) 70
Vestorin, Inez (wife of S. Cavio) 90
Vicarias, Juana (wife of D. Arnau) 97
Vicenta, Isabela Casilda (wife of L. Rodriguez) 79
Victori [Victoria, Victorina],
  Clara (wife of J. Nielo) 108
  Ignes 15
  Inez (wife of S. Cavedo) 74, 77, 90
Vidata, Maria Ana (wife of J. Trutilon) 99
Villa, Agata 18
  Agueda (wife of P. Vivas) 98
  Ana 19
  Antonia (wife of A. Roger) 25, 96
  Antonia Fiol 91, 99
  Catalina (wife of B. Mula) 86
  Francisco 49, 95, 96, 105
  Juana 18, 19, 45, 84, 91
  Juana (wife of F. Pallicer/Pallerin) 19, 84, 105, 114
  Juana 18
  Juana (wife of M. Ponz) 18, 91
  Margarita 18, 99
  Margarita (wife of S.Coll) 17, 99
  Maria 95
  Maria (wife of J. Lorenzo) 22, 95
  Maria Ana 18
  Maria Ana Cardona 18
  Maria Ferrer 95, 96, 105
  Pablo 9
  Pedro 91, 99
Villalonga, Agueda 16, 22, 90
  Agueda (wife of B. Segui), 14, 84, 90
  Agueda Melia 84, 90
  Bartolome 84, 90
  Catalina (wife of B. Mula) 97

Index

Villalonga (cont'd)
   Francisca 22, 97
   Francisco 49
   Juan 51, 90
   Margarita (wife of J. Costa) 90
   Maria 90
   Mariana Cardona 90
   Martina 16, 97
   Miguel 22, 44, 97
   Rafaela 22, 97
   Rafaela Mercadal 22
Villan, Joseph Maria de Jesus Geron 5
Villegas, Barbara (wife of J. Llanez) 76
   Catarina 21
   Esperanza 21
Villi [Billy], 37
Vimenes, Jose 143
Vinz, Juana (wife of M. Vivos) 91
Vincent, Eliza 146
   Mary (wife of J. Sharp) 147
Vivas [Vives, Vivos], Agueda Villa 98
   Antonia 98
   Juana Vinz 91
   Magino 91
   Margarita (wife of J. Pratts) 91
   Margarita (wife of S. Prast) 19
   Victoria (wife of D. Hernandez) 10, 87, 98
Volantin, Lucia 150

W

Walton [Wanton], Edward 32, 37, 129
Wardlow, Juan 131
Waterman, Elioza 133
Watson, Maria 99
   Pedro 99
Wedington, Alecia (wife of S. Rodriguez) 75
Welon, Juan 92
   Juana Allon 92

Welon (cont'd)
   Maria Josefa 92
Welsh, Ana Bowin 86
   Guillermo 86
   Juana (wife of A. Leslie) 86
   Maria (wife of T. Fleming) 73
White, ——
   Regina Maria 5
Whitmore, Roberto 61
Wickes, Bernardo 145
   Isak 117
   Mary Kunan 145
Wiedman, Felipe 124, 126
Wiggens, Juana 151
   Patty 148
Wildes, Nathaniel 133
Wilson, Hana (wife of R. Nelson) 100
   Samuel 67
Win, Margarita (wife of P. MacFeal) 73
Witen [Witter], Francisco 80
   Gualtero 5
   Juan Bautista 80
   Maria Rafaela 80
Woodland, Margarita 103

X

Xeres, Ana (wife of S. Hortega) 90
Ximenes [Ximinez, Ximines]
   Andres 84
   Barbara Ponz 92
   Catarina 20, 92
   Catalina Espineta 93
   Esperanza 20, 93
   Geronima 93
   Jose [Josef] 143
   Juan 92, 107
   Juana (wife of A. Baya) 92
   Juana (wife of J. Triay) 20
   Juana (wife of S. Triay) 92

Index

Ximenes (cont'd)
  Juana Pallicer 84
  Maria 20, 92, 93, 144
  Maria Ramalera 20, 92, 93
  Miguel 84
  Rafael 20, 92, 93
  Rafaela 92, 92, 93
  Rosa Clavero 84

Y

Yonge, Enrique 149
  Felipe Roberto 141
  Maria Atkinson 149
Youngblood, Jesse 68

Z

Zamorano [Samorano],
  Francisca 77
  Francisco 77
  Francisco del Corral 77
  Gonzales 77
  Gregorio 34
  Joaquin Gonzales 77
  Joseph 34
  Juan 34
  Juan Josef de Sa—gun 77
  Maria de la O. 77
  Petrona 77
Zans [see Sans]
Zuares [see Suarez]

Donna Rachal Mills

Mills's own roots go deep into the Floridas—embracing Spaniards, Frenchmen, Gypsies, Indians, and Celtic-American traders who explored the breadth of the eighteenth-century Gulf, tilled its soil, produced its families, and reclaimed it from the British during the course of the American Revolution.

A resident of Naples (Florida, of course) and a Certified Genealogical Record Searcher since 1985, Mills also holds a B. A. in Historic Preservation from the University of Alabama and an M.A. in Architectural History from the University of Virginia. Following the footsteps of her ancestors, she has explored Southern courthouses and archives since the age of ten.

www.ingramcontent.com/pod-product-compliance
Lightning Source LLC
Chambersburg PA
CBHW051923160426
43198CB00012B/2012